Law, Security and Migration

This book analyzes the impact of the increasing securitization of migration within the international legal and political order.

Migration has increasingly become a security issue. Examining this tendency towards the securitization of migration around the world, this book argues that it is indicative of a shift in the international order towards geopolitical and security strategies, and away from cooperation and multilateralism. States are now more inclined to produce national legislation in the fields of countering terrorism, migration, and security, than dealing with such global issues through international cooperation and international norm-making. As such, this book demonstrates, they tend to prioritize national rather than international interests in a radical shift away from the universal rights and liberal values that were dominant at the end of the 20th century, to a model based on geopolitical interests. The securitization of migration is a process that not only affects the rights of migrants, but ushers in a new international legal and political order.

This book will be of considerable interest to scholars and professionals in the fields of international law, international relations, migration, security, and human rights.

Laura Planas Gifra is Postdoctoral Fellow in Law at Pompeu Fabra University and the University of Barcelona, Spain.

Law, Security and Migration

The Nationalistic Turn in the International Order

Laura Planas Gifra

Routledge
Taylor & Francis Group
a GlassHouse Book

First published 2025
by Routledge
4 Park Square, Milton Park, Abingdon, Oxon OX14 4RN

and by Routledge
605 Third Avenue, New York, NY 10158

Routledge is an imprint of the Taylor & Francis Group, an informa business

A GlassHouse book

British Library Cataloguing-in-Publication Data
A catalogue record for this book is available from the British Library

Library of Congress Cataloging-in-Publication Data
Names: Planas Gifra, Laura, 1993– author.
Title: Law, security and migration : the nationalistic turn in the international order / Laura Planas Gifra.
Description: Abingdon, Oxon [UK] ; New York, NY : Routledge, 2025. | Includes bibliographical references and index.
Identifiers: LCCN 2024025467 (print) | LCCN 2024025468 (ebook) | ISBN 9781032602165 (hardback) | ISBN 9781032602226 (paperback) | ISBN 9781003458159 (ebook)
Subjects: LCSH: Emigration and immigration law. | Emigration and immigration—Security measures. | Border security—Law and legislation. | National security—Law and legislation. | Security, International.
Classification: LCC K3275 .P537 2025 (print) | LCC K3275 (ebook) | DDC 342.08/2—dc23/eng/20240612
LC record available at https://lccn.loc.gov/2024025467
LC ebook record available at https://lccn.loc.gov/2024025468

ISBN: 9781032602165 (hbk)
ISBN: 9781032602226 (pbk)
ISBN: 9781003458159 (ebk)

DOI: 10.4324/9781003458159

Typeset in Sabon
by Apex CoVantage, LLC

Contents

Acronyms

Asian Infrastructure Investment Bank	(AIIB)
Australian Federal Police	(AFP)
Australian Security Intelligence Organization	(ASIO)
Brazil, Russia, India, China, and South Africa	(BRICS)
Clear Law Enforcement for Criminal Alien Removal Act	(CLEAR)
Crimes Against the State Unit of South Africa	(CATS)
Department of Homeland Security	(DHS)
European Counter Terrorism Centre	(ECTC)
Euskadi Ta Askatasuna	(ETA)
Global Security Initiative	(GSI)
Immigration and Naturalization Service	(INS)
Inter-American Commission on Human Rights	(IACHR)
International Energy Agency	(IEA)
International Labor Organization	(ILO)
International Organization for Migration	(IOM)
Irish Republican Army	(IRA)
National Crime Information Center	(NCIC)
National Security Entry-Exit Registration System	(NSEERS)
Non-Governmental Organization	(NGO)
North Atlantic Treaty Organization	(NATO)
Operation Sovereign Borders	(OSB)
Organisation of African Unity	(OAU)
Private Military and Security Company	(PMSC)
Protection of Constitutional Democracy Against Terrorist and Related Activities Ac	(POCDATARA)
Shanghai Cooperation Organization	(SCO)
South African Police Service	(SAPS)
Special Air Service	(SAS)
Tracking Refugees Information System	(TRIS)
Treaty on the Functioning of the European Union	(TFEU)

United Nations High Commissioner for Refugees	(UNHCR)
United States Refugee Admissions Program	(USRAP)
Uniting and Strengthening America by Providing Appropriate Tools Required to Intercept and Obstruct Terrorism (more commonly referred to as the USA Patriot Act or PATRIOT Act)	

Acknowledgements

This book has been written in tumultuous times, with nations fighting battles, feeling the consequences of the climate crisis, and with peoples around the world fleeing from conflicts, hunger, poverty, and devastation. It is during noisy times that those bringing calm and wisdom help to withstand uncertainty. The people I thank here have showed me new ways to see the world, helped me understand an era marked by changes, and given me the courage to work on this manuscript.

I give thanks foremost to the director of my doctoral thesis, Pablo Pareja Alcaraz, who shared his enthusiasm about my research and supported all my endeavors. I could not have imagined in my last years at law school that the supervisor of my undergraduate thesis would years later also become my PhD supervisor and guide me into the world of academia. There have been countless meetings and conversations, and I am grateful for each one of them. I give further thanks to the Faculty of Law at Pompeu Fabra University and its academic staff for the time spent as an undergraduate and doctoral student.

I also owe deep gratitude to Andreu Olesti Rayo, who opened the doors of the Faculty of Law at the University of Barcelona, and who has been a cornerstone since our first encounter. He has offered valuable counsel and advice and has genuinely and truthfully embraced my work as a researcher. This book has been written during my time as a postdoctoral researcher at the University of Barcelona. I am grateful for all the opportunities and the support this institution has given me.

The evolution of the book owes much to the time spent at the Max Planck Institute for Comparative Public Law and International Law. It was in this institution where I met Malcolm Jorgensen, who lent a helping hand from the very beginning. I am indebted to his selfless assistance reviewing draft chapters and providing valuable comments.

I am privileged to have been able to share so many thoughts, fears, and laughs with my colleagues Marcia Rodrigues and Gastón Medici. I am filled with gratitude for their empathy and sensitivity and feel lucky that the time spent together as colleagues at the University of Barcelona has evolved into such meaningful friendships.

I am forever indebted to my parents for instilling in me the value of education and giving me the chance to study and learn for so long. They are the ones who taught me the importance of being well-informed, thinking critically, and seeing the world from different perspectives. There is still an entire life to continue learning, and I am grateful for being able to follow this pathway thanks to them. I am also thankful to my brother, Joan, for believing in my goals and never seeing limits to the dreams I wanted to pursue. To my nephew, Jaume, and niece, Helena, for bringing so much joy to life. And finally, to my husband, Joan, for bringing calm to the mind and happiness to the heart since the very first day our paths crossed.

Introduction

A vision of securitization in international relations

The work of this book emerges from a doctoral thesis, where I studied securitization practices in the field of migration. These pages are not a re-worked thesis but are instead a continuation of the debate that emerged from it. The thesis represented a starting point to connect the securitization of migration to a wider sphere of international relations, that in relation to the international order and the changes it was undergoing. There were signs of new tensions between powers, the disengagement of the United States as a global leader, new international conflicts arising, and non-military factors becoming more relevant for geopolitical purposes. National security has been at the center of concern for many states, moving away from human security and the protection of a global community threatened by wars, environmental disasters, and health security issues. Instead, the nation seems to be once more the main unit of concern. The regulation of migration has become yet another area of preoccupation, one showing this disentanglement from the protection of international human rights, and where new priorities are those in relation to controlling and refraining incoming migration flows.

This is my perception of how the world is changing and it is the vision reflected in this book. While I am not a realist, in these pages I argue that there have been certain strategies and practices by states moving towards a prioritization for national security, geopolitical calculations, and military action. While this may seem contradictory, my personal view is that it is not. This book is intended to serve as a tool to raise awareness of these changes and alert of their potential consequences. It presents migration as another sign that the liberal international order as we have known it in the past decades is changing. Instead of seeing migration as an enrichment for society and multiculturalism in a more than ever interconnected world, migration is seen as a threat to the nation and presented as a threat to society. Instead of helping those in need fleeing from conflict, hunger, and devastation, we are building barriers to prevent them from coming to 'our' territories. While the new century could have been marked by the prevalence of democracy, human rights and freedoms, and human security, it has instead gradually moved to the opposite direction. Therefore, I see this confrontation between the realist views expressed in the book and its goal to raise awareness against a realist vision of the international system not as opposing forces, but instead as intriguing and necessary.

My wish is to contribute to current debates by offering a new vision of this changing order through the lens of migration, a highly mistreated area. Migrants have been pointed at as potential terrorists and criminals, as the source for economic burdens, and the reason for cutbacks in some welfare systems. They are unfoundedly blamed for a wide range of issues at destination countries. But we need not forget that many of those moving from their homes today are fleeing for their lives in search of security for them and their families. I hope this book serves as motor to call for a change of direction and combat these new tendencies, while upholding the importance of preserving human security.

An uncertain future

In recent years debates on the crisis of the global order as we know it have multiplied, leaving many to wonder what the future will look like, if power structures will change, or what values will prevail. What is more, since the start of the war between Russia and Ukraine, some contend that this change has already begun, and that a new geopolitical age has finally emerged.

But this change has left a few signs over the years, as our century has been marked by a complex succession of events: the terrorist attacks of 9/11 in the United States, the 2008 financial crisis, and a global pandemic, just to mention a few. These episodes have led to changes in the functioning of the international system, and it is important to understand why they are occurring and what they may lead to. One of the most important dynamics has been the failure of the United States and Europe to establish a world liberal international system. These countries wanted to enhance financial institutions and reinforce liberal values, human rights, and democratic systems. However, China has emerged as a superpower posing a threat to the hegemonic leadership of the US, and precisely counteracting the so-called liberal system. China has seen the Western defense of liberal values as an abuse of the mandate to maintain international order, and as a way to interfere into the national affairs of countries where the US may have a national interest. As the United States used the terrorist threat as an argument to invade Iraq and Afghanistan, other countries have seen this as a strategic move to interfere in the domestic affairs and functioning of third countries in the name of democracy. This has led many countries to follow an old vision of great powers based on the Westphalian model instead of being drawn by the intentions of the West. Recognizing these moves is important for scholars in the field to try to predict the impact of these changes and the consequences for future relations between states.

Russia is an example of the grounding force of unilateralism and of the resistance of a Westphalian understanding of geopolitics. Even though with the end of the Cold War the country was placed at a second stage and was never able to supersede US supremacy, it has nevertheless demonstrated many times its capacity to destabilize the international order. It has meddled in US elections, illegally annexed Crimea, backed Bashar al-Assad in Syria, been involved in the assassination of enemies in Britain and Germany, and after increasing tensions in Ukraine by deliberately destabilizing the country and threatening to occupy it, it finally started a war in the region in February 2022. Since World War II, military conflict among great powers had been absent, but Russia decided to put an end to this dynamic. Putin already said it in 2019: "the liberal idea" had "outlived its purpose" (Barber et al., 2019). Or more clearly: "This liberal idea presupposes that nothing needs to be done. That migrants can kill, plunder and rape without impunity because their rights as migrants must be protected. . . . Every crime must have its punishment. The liberal idea has become obsolete" (Barber et al., 2019). Thence somehow, Russia's attacks to invade Ukraine have shown that the Westphalian model is still going strong. And as a consequence to Russian actions, its neighboring states have been afraid of the country's future intentions towards them. They have been put on guard, and even Germany reversed decades of military hesitancy and spent 100 billion euros in its defense budget right away (Cave, 2022). Similarly, the European Union followed by agreeing to "resolutely bolster investment" in defense capabilities and substantially increase defense spending (Brzozowski, 2022). As Cave puts it "Ukraine may also be just the first of several tests for the old order" (Cave, 2022).

The European Union has seen Russia's war on Ukraine as a landmark in its history, and as EU leaders gathered in a summit in the former royal palace of Versailles in Paris in March 2022, they decided to "collectively rearm and become autonomous in food, energy and military hardware" (Boffey, 2022). France, with President Emmanuel Macron, has been pushing the region to become more autonomous, but some EU Member States – especially those with economic liberal ideas and strong ties with countries outside of the EU zone – have been reluctant to this idea, fearing that protectionism would end up becoming the new model (Leali & Moens, 2022; Boffey, 2022). While it remains to be seen what the outcome of the Versailles declaration will be in practice, the Russia-Ukraine conflict has become a turning point for the EU and has forced its institutions to take a more critical look at its dependency on third countries and to invest more in defense technologies. The possibility of the EU becoming a more independent region than before certainly reinforces this idea that a return to a model based on geopolitics and self-protection may be on its way to being established. And on top of that, the European

Union – a symbol of liberal democracy during the past decades – has seen the failure of the Treaty for Establishing a Constitution for Europe because of the French and Dutch rejections, Great Britain left the EU in 2020, and xenophobic right-wing parties have grown and become more powerful across European countries (Mearsheimer, 2019).

What is more, while Western countries have wanted liberal democracy to be the system to be spread around the world, the truth is that democratic states have been disappearing in the last decade, dropping from 42 countries in 2012 to 34 in 2022 (Boese et al., 2022). Recent conflicts showing this decay are the coup d'état in Myanmar, and the Taliban takeover of Afghanistan after American troops left the country. On another note, former President Donald J. Trump returned to unilateralism through his "America first" because he thought that the United States was a victim rather than a beneficiary of the "rules-based order" (Cave, 2022). Even if the presidency of Joe Biden has tried to go back to a more multilateralist system in terms of international politics, the world is now looking at the country with hesitancy, doubting if its government will be able to take the leadership it once had, with China dipping its toes, and Russia seeking to expand its territory across boundaries. If there were already a debate on whether a new world order was emerging well before Russia's latest military actions in Ukraine, the world is now watching how a new era of great power conflict with a new global order has already begun.[1]

China and India have gained relevance within the international system. They have high population numbers, they have an exponential GDP growth, and they are two of the few nuclear powers existing in the world. Furthermore, China has projects such as the Belt and Road Initiative and the Silk Road to further extend its power across regions. Russia, from its side, has never been too keen on the international order established by the United States after the end of the Cold War, and it has tried to challenge US hegemony and the universalization of liberal values which have been imposed on the international system. Conflicts like those of the South China Sea or the Arctic show the importance that territory still has today and potential interstate conflicts that may more violently arise in the future. These states dispute the world as it has been understood in the past decades and are calling for a revision of the world order, on the fundamentals it is based on, and on the powers dominating it.

Powerful changes in the dynamics of international security and the confrontation between globalization and regionalization processes are part of the equation. But the effects of the Trump administration in the United States

1 Ignacio Ramonet, in his article "Una nuevad edad geopolítica" for *Le Monde Diplomatique* argued that February 24, 2022, the date of the start of the Ukranian war, was the landmark for a new geopolitical era.

marked by an anti-multilateral approach of international relations and the partial decay of the European Union with the Brexit also show a turmoil within the West's hegemony, and especially on the role and impact of the United States. The United Nations has been unable to respond to the Russia-Ukraine crisis, another sign of the molder of the widest international organization bringing states together to promote global peace and security.

Altogether, it remains to be seen whether the liberal order will be able to survive, if it will fall against a new realist order, or whether both will coexist together – one led by the United States, and another led by China. While it is true that some states might have profited from these moral standards to intervene in the national affairs of third countries, these are still important to maintain a world based on the protection of the individual. And a world in which human security is put at the forefront of international agendas should be defended. It is with democratic values and with international cooperation to tackle insecurity that during the 1990s and 2000s wars downgraded to their lowest level since the end of World War II. Human security should then be at the center of concern, and that can only happen in an order based on the promotion of international peace and security, the protection of fundamental rights, and the spread of democratic values across countries.

Migration in the midst of a changing era

Amid these changes, migration movements and the terrorist threat have also become two of the most important phenomena of the past decades and are shaping the new security strategies of many states and the international system as a whole. Rising climate and environmental concerns and civil and interstate conflicts affect peoples' lives and force them to leave their homes. Whichever the reason of their departure, there are many today trying to find better lives abroad. This has stressed the international system as the regime governing migration has shown unable to adapt to the escalation of migratory flows. No state can successfully manage migration by itself, which at the same time leads to tensions between countries.

In the second half of 2015, with the escalation of the conflict in Syria, thousands of its citizens left looking for protection in Europe, leaving its homes devastated by war. Because of these increasing migratory flows and the growing terrorist threat, a considerable number of individuals – particularly those sharing populist and right-wing ideas – have seen these refugees and asylum seekers as 'invaders'. Altogether, this century, with the events of September 11 and the Syrian refugee crisis, has been marked by the extension of the idea that irregular migration is a security threat; one that needs to be resolved through security strategies.

The securitization of migration has been in part a response to massive refugee flows and the incapacity of Western countries to cope with increasing numbers of immigration and, as states have widely defended, a response to the terrorist threat. Discourses on the latter line have linked migration and national security in the past years and have consolidated the perception among a big part of the population that migration can be a threat to the economic, social, and cultural progress of the country, leading to rising extremist right-wing discourses on the negative impact of immigration. The establishment of this relationship between migration and security has pursued self-interested political purposes, as it has been used to legitimize privileged positions (Karyotis, 2007; Messina, 2014) and approve measures that would otherwise be hard to implement. Accepting an issue such as immigration as a common security threat can become an opportunity for politicians to reinforce collective identification and generate greater loyalties (Boswell, 2007). It is therefore of utmost importance to detect when this happens and ensure that the rights of the most vulnerable are protected.

One of the biggest 'justifications' to securitize migration has been the terrorist threat. And even though most terrorist organizations are concentrated in the Middle East because its violence has reached other regions in the world, some have started seeing "outsiders" with a particular ethnic profile as potential threats. Terrorism has been one of the most violent phenomena in recent years, and after each and every attack, citizens are scared and expect the state to protect them. This has led many countries to create security measures specifically directed to counter the terrorist threat, but also directed to contending migration. Migration and terrorism have thus been dealt with as one interrelated issue as this is the way they have been presented since the 9/11 events. And as massive refugee flows fleeing from conflict have at the same time widely spread and the states' reception systems have been overflooded, the securitization of migration has been the magic potion to regain control over borders and migration.

Furthermore, since the perpetrators of these attacks match a specific ethnic profile (Karyotis, 2011), migrants have been associated with rising existential threats, which has also placed them at the core of many national security agendas. The securitization of migration is the result of a process which brings migration – which is typically not a security issue – to the security arena. As a result of political elite and mass media discourses, new laws and public policies bringing migration closer to national security have been enacted around the world, and the counter-terrorist discourse has shown to be a powerful one to justify this association. Migrants are thus blamed for aggravating economic crises and threatening our cultures. But after terrorist attacks, they are also held accountable for these massacres, reinforcing the image that the terrorist is one with a particular ethnicity or religion.

This does not mean that all citizens are convinced by the negative discourses offered by certain political groups and ideologies. However, what seems to be clear is that anti-immigrant sentiments have grown in the past years, as countries have faced economic and security difficulties. Part of the population has indeed believed these arguments. They have been convinced that their well-being and the welfare state were threatened by the arrival of immigrant – and particularly refugee – flows. Thence it is important to make impartial studies analyzing the objectiveness of these threats and to continue producing academic literature demystifying these ideas to protect the rights of all.

The terrorist threat has made states become very defensive, and as a result they are increasing national security measures. This threat has been used to justify a set of legislative amendments, the passing of contentious public policies, and even more controversial foreign strategies. Technological advancements have enabled governments to further control their populations, which has somehow diminished the privacy rights of the citizenry based on protecting from the terrorist threat. Even more, vulnerable groups such as migrants, and especially refugees, have seen a deterioration of their rights as states have kept on increasing border control and implementing administrative barriers. At the same time, extremist anti-immigrant discourses against the immigrant population have spread, making it even more difficult for them to integrate in their new host countries. On top of that, they have been often accused of participating in terrorist attacks in the West, which has worsened their adaptability conditions in these countries.

The attacks of September 11 became an important landmark for Western nations to create a strong linkage between the terrorist threat and migration. However, the Bali bombings or the Mombasa and Kenya attacks have also been altogether a good justification to connect national security to a borders-related issue beyond the West. But other economic and social discourses have also been used, as populism, nationalism, and far-right ideologies have increasingly taken the stage in the past years. Therefore, discourses other than that related to terrorism have also paved the way to establish securitization practices in the field of migration in nations around the world. This explains why we have seen a proliferation of legislation in the field of immigration reinforcing a perceived 'need' to protect from external threats.

Altogether, these practices in both Western and non-Western nations show once again that a return to a realist model is on its way. This book seeks to humbly contribute to the academic literature by offering a different perspective on how different spheres – that of national security and migration – have slowly shown a move towards a realist approach to international relations. The securitization of migration is thence another sign of the changes within the international order and a partial return to a geopolitical model based on prioritizing national security over human security. We seem to be leaving the liberal framework to return to a Westphalian system.

This return to a more realist model does not necessarily mean that the entire system will change and that all actors will base their actions fully based on geopolitics. There can still be liberal states pushing for the maintenance of cosmopolitism. We are still yet to see whether the two movements will coexist together or whether one of them will prevail over the other. However, the point of this book is to show that with different securitizing practices – such as it is the case with migration – the comeback of Westphalian geopolitics is slowly becoming a reality. Only time will tell what the international order will look like in the years to come.

Therefore, this book wants to answer two central questions: First, how is migration securitized? And second, can these measures be a sign that the international order is changing?

As some authors contend, there has been a Western dominance of the study of international relations (Acharya & Buzan, 2017). In the case of securitization theory, which initially emerged at the Copenhagen School, this has also been said to reflect a Western vision (Vuori, 2008; Wilkinson, 2007; Ezeokafor & Kaunert, 2018). In this sense and responding to the need to study securitization beyond the West, Vuori (2008) applied securitization to non-democratic states, and Ezeokafor and Kaunert (2018) shifted the focus to neo-patrimonial states in Africa. This book also seeks going beyond this Western perspective, and that is why it analyzes securitization practices of various states, located throughout all continents, with the intent to reflect a potentially more global perspective. With that in mind, and in order to offer a global view on securitization practices in the field of migration, part II will study securitization measures in the Americas, Europe, Asia, Oceania, the Middle East, and Africa. For each of these regions, different cases have been selected to understand how the securitization of migration has been carried out and which are the legal and policy measures dealing with migration through national security.

At the theoretical level, bringing this analysis to the world of international relations will be useful to contribute to the debate on the changes of the international order. As theorists scrutinize the consequences of the rise of China, the reasons why an anti-multilateralist like Donald Trump won the presidency of the United States, or the consequences of the war by Russia on Ukraine, questions on whether the world as we know it today will change have emerged. From my point of view, the study of securitization processes would fit within this debate to try to explain whether these securitization processes can also be a sign of the prioritization for bringing non-typical security issues to the security arena, and to solve them through the lens of national security. A proof that the system is changing towards a more realist than liberal one.

If societies base their national identities on race, ethnicity, or religion, and exclude those who are different, conflict is more likely to arise. In a world where globalization has facilitated transportation, communication technologies, and migratory movements, societies are becoming more diverse. But we need to see this diversity as a cultural enrichment, not as a social threat. Instead, the application of securitization measures in a wide range of countries has become rather common, which shows that states are framing migrants as a security threat. Higher border controls, restricting access to healthcare, and imposing difficulties for them to formalize their legal status in hosting countries are just some of the signs that universal democratic values have not completely overcome the realist vision of the state, in which maintaining national security is what is most important and where geopolitics shape security agendas. And when the protection of the individual – and not the state – is the goal of national and international security strategies, when enough people reject liberal principles, the order cannot be maintained.

This book seeks to put an eye on securitization processes to emphasize the importance of maintaining human security and the protection of particularly vulnerable groups, such as that of migrants. It wants to shed light on the relevance of securing the fundamental values in which democracy is formed: international human rights and freedoms. International institutions and multilateral cooperation can help protect these values while adjusting economic liberalism so that it addresses inequalities more effectively. But what is more, it humbly wants to enlighten the importance of building a sense of common belonging to show that the idea of the nation-state is not incompatible with that of diversity, so that we can build societies centered on the ideas of equity, equality, and non-discrimination. Because global cosmopolitanism cares about the peoples in the world, no matter where they are from or what their beliefs are. And national frontiers can be compatible with the idea that we are all citizens of the world.

Overview

In this book I will argue that the securitization of migration is compounded by a series of laws and policies which have been spread in many countries around the world, and, because of their restrictive nature, their proliferation can be seen as another sign that the international order as we have known it since the end of the Cold War is changing. While there have been several studies on securitization, the novelty that this book would like to bring is precisely on the latter part. Its importance lies in its transversal nature. As the book will show, the dispersing of insecurities has political and social consequences, which can also be extrapolated to the international security. Within this international sphere, the development of international law is not as frequent or efficient as before, and states are less keen to be bound by new international norms. And in a world where global issues are spreading, states are dealing with international security threats through the lens of national security instead of multilateral cooperation.

The book is divided into two parts. The first part deals with more theoretical frameworks, while the second proposes a series of case studies. Before getting into the heart of the study, Chapters 1 and 2 will initially focus on current debates on the changing international order and the influence of international law within the new order that is being built. This will be useful to present the current situation and discussions on how the order has changed during this century. Chapter 3 presents the merits of adopting a constructivist perspective in the field of migration and security, going through the concept of securitization. Chapter 4 will go deeper into the object of analysis and engage with the analysis of securitization practices and how these actions are showing a move by states to the direction of national security prevalence. The second part of the book will examine the cases of the United States and Mexico in the Americas (Chapter 5); the European Union (Chapter 6); Indonesia, Malaysia, and Australia in Asia and Oceania (Chapter 7); and of Saudi Arabia, Qatar, and South Africa in the Middle East and Africa (Chapter 8). In the concluding chapter, I return to the debate of dealing with migration through a security perspective and how this affects the rights of migrants, while questioning the threat to liberal values that these actions entail.

I do not intend this book to be a history of international relations, nor a description of what the international order will look like in the future. There are dozens of important writers who have contributed to these debates with far greater experience and wisdom. Instead, the purpose here is to focus on the role of the securitization of migration in these changing times. The book at hand is written in a period of turmoil, in times of spreading conflict, and increasing critiques towards the so-called liberal order. This book thence wants to raise awareness on the consequences of focusing only on maintaining national security and failing to provide security to vulnerable individuals, while expressing the importance of maintaining democratic values and human rights. Above all, it seeks to shed some light to these dark times of uncertainty by encouraging the construction of an era where human security prevails.

References

Acharya, A., & Buzan, B. (2017). Why is there no non-western international relations theory? ten years on. *International Relations of the Asia-Pacific*, *17*(3), 341–370.

Barber, L., Foy, H., & Barker, A. (2019, June 28). Vladimir Putin says liberalism has 'become obsolete'. *Financial Times*. Retrieved January 29, 2024, from www.ft.com/content/670039ec-98f3-11e9-9573-ee5cbb98ed36

Boese, V. A., Alizada, N., Lundstedt, M., Morrison, K., Natsika, N., Sato, Y., Tai, H., & Lindberg, S. I. (2022). Autocratization changing nature? Democracy report 2022. *Varieties of Democracy Institute*. Retrieved January 30, 2024, from https://v-dem.net/media/publications/dr_2022.pdf

Boffey, D. (2022, March 11). EU leaders announce intention to collectively rearm in face of Putin threat. *The Guardian*. Retrieved January 22, 2024, from www.theguardian.com/world/2022/mar/11/eu-leaders-announce-intention-collectively-rearm-putin-threat-russia-ukraine

Boswell, C. (2007). Migration control in Europe after 9/11: Explaining the absence of securitisation. *Journal of Common Market Studies*, *45*(3), 589–610.

Brzozowski, A. (2022, March 11). With war at its doorstep, EU agrees to move on defence. *Euractiv*. www.euractiv.com/section/defence-and-security/news/with-war-at-its-doorstep-eu-agrees-to-move-on-defence/

Cave, D. (2022, March 6). The war in Ukraine holds a warning for the world order. *The New York Times*. Retrieved January 29, 2024, from www.nytimes.com/2022/03/04/world/ukraine-russia-war-authoritarianism.html

Ezeokafor, E., & Kaunert, C. (2018). Securitization outside of the west. *Global Discourse: An Interdisciplinary Journal of Current Affairs and Applied Contemporary Thought (Global Discourse)*, *8*(1), 83–99.

Karyotis, G. (2007). European migration policy in the aftermath of September 11: The security-migration nexus. *Innovation: The European Journal of Social Science Research*, *20*(1), 1–17.

Leali, G., & Moens, B. (2022, March 9). Ukraine war gives Macron's drive for EU autonomy new impetus. *Politico*. www.politico.eu/article/war-in-ukraine-versailles-france-emmanuel-macrons-strategic-autonomy/

Mearsheimer, J. (2019). Bound to fail: The rise and fall of the liberal international order. *International Security*, *43*(4), 7–50.

Messina, A. (2014). Securitizing immigration in the age of terror. *World Politics*, *66*(3), 530–559.

Vuori, J. (2008). Illocutionary logic and strands of securitization: Applying the theory of securitization to the study of non-democratic political orders. *European Journal of International Relations*, *14*(1), 65–99.

Wilkinson, C. (2007). The Copenhagen School on tour in Kyrgyzstan: Is securitization theory useable outside Europe. *Security Dialogue*, *38*(1), 5–25.

Part 1

Migration and security in the 21st century

1

A changing international order

The modern state in international relations

It is crucial to recognize the different schools of international relations when referring to the international order. That is why this chapter will start by offering an overview of international relations studies through the schools of realism and liberalism, to then analyze the impact that these have on the international order. Once a theoretical framework is set, then the chapter will move on to specify what this international order looked like in the aftermath of the Cold War and the changes it undertook after 9/11. As it will be shown, since 2001 and to this day, there have been a series of events that have led to the adoption of national security measures which prioritize the adoption of unilateral actions to address international concerns, instead of multilateral efforts. Altogether this leads to current debates on whether and why the international order is changing, and what these changes will entail.

As put by Carr (1951), one of the problems with liberal internationalism is that it cannot succeed because the international order is one with an anarchic nature. This implies that cooperation will always be problematic and that international institutions will never be strong enough. But he also questioned the postulates upon which the liberal international order is based, wondering if these are bankrupt, and arguing that realism can also offer social transformation (Molloy, 2021). While this was written in the 1950s, today discussions from a realist perspective have reappeared.

In international relations, political realism maintains that states will always compete for power because the more power one has, the more likely it is to survive. When this competition becomes too intense, inter-state conflict is likely to arise, which can even turn into an armed conflict. According to this view, the structure of the international system is always one based on gaining more power and making geopolitical calculations. More concretely, realism is based on different assumptions. Firstly, states are the only actors and there is no authority above them. Secondly, they want to expand their power and their ultimate goal is to maintain their own security to survive in the system. Thirdly, they can never be certain of the real intentions of other

DOI: 10.4324/9781003458159-2

actors in the system. Lastly, they act according to calculations and assessments of each other and make rational decisions accordingly. That is, they all have different capabilities and resources, and they act in consonance to them, always prioritizing their own national interests. Critics of realism argue that this is a traditional ideology that has become "old-fashioned" and cannot be useful to explain contemporary conflicts. Nevertheless, this theoretical framework has proven to be remarkably resilient when dealing with issues of international security.

On the other side of the spectrum, there is liberalism, a doctrine that has been developed with the ideas of intellectuals like Adam Smith, Jeremy Bentham, and Immanuel Kant. There are different ways to describe liberalism, and this can be divided into a range of visions, but here the term will be used following Fukuyama's (2022a) description. According to his view, liberalism is based on the limitation of the power of governments through law and the creation of institutions protecting the rights of individuals. It is a doctrine that can encompass a wide range of political views, so long as these agree on the "foundational importance of equal individual rights, law, and freedom" (Fukuyama, 2022a).

As with realism, there is no single unified liberal theory as such. But there are certain elements that are common in all its developments. Liberalism focuses on human reason, progress, and freedom to contribute to international peace and security. Thus, it is seen as a way to prevent conflict. This argument is supported by its three core foundations, as claimed by the works of Paine (1791/1992) and Kant (1795/1991). First, this is because liberal democracies are keener to solve problems in peaceful ways and are less likely to initiate conflict with other democracies. Second, liberalism promotes international trade. This promotes economic growth, but it also acts as an additional element to avoid conflict, as international commerce generates state interdependence and thus refrains states from wanting to find themselves involved in disputes with their partners. Lastly, liberalism promotes individual rights, equality, and human dignity. The individual is free to make its own choices, including in the political realms. And these individual rights are guarded by international institutions.

No international order lasts forever (Mearsheimer, 2019), and the world has seen a series of changes over time which have moved the international order from one to another. New great powers may emerge, and these powers may replace a dominant ideology, or a hegemonic power may lose its dominance. In sum, there are many ways in which the international order may change. What seems to be the dominant discourse today is that this order is in fact changing.

Understanding world order

To talk about the world order and how it is changing it is first necessary to define it. There are two ways to look at the world order, an analytical one and a prescriptive one. Both usages are useful to understand and grasp the realities of international political life at a global level.

According to Amitav Acharya (2007), an empirical cognition of international relations would define it as the relations between the main actors within an international system, including both state and non-state actors. This initial vision would be used to describe power distribution among actors and the framework for the conduct of diplomacy and international relations on a global scale. However, a more prescriptive view would define world order as the preferred arrangement of power and authority, a 'desired' state of world. In this case, world order would be associated with the realization that values such as peace, economic growth, and human rights should be the fundamental basis of global politics. This concept is key for the study of international relations but is also crucial to determine the lens through which to view and understand global developments and foreign policy choices.

The distinguishing characteristic of an order is that it is settled, structured, the opposite of chaos (Mazarr et al., 2016). Ikenberry (2001) defines it as a set of "governing arrangements between states, including its fundamental rules, principles, and institutions". Similarly, Barnett (2021) defines it as the way in which rules, institutions, law, and norms produce and maintain relations and actions. Therefore, even as the idea of an international order does not necessarily involve coherence (Schweller, 2001), it does presume a structured pattern of relations (Mazarr et al., 2016). The idea is different from that of an international system, which is the global context in which states operate, pushing them to interact in certain ways (Waltz, 1979). This idea of an order based on a structure founded by and reigned by institutions, rules, and law will be the basis for my conceptualization of international order.

It is inescapable that most Western scholars perceive world order through the lenses of a Western approach which sets the Treaty of Westphalia of 1648 as a landmark. This has been treated as the beginning of the modern world and premised on the emergence of the state as a sovereign unit and the dominant political actor. However, this world order had a clear Eurocentric nature and conceived Western states as hierarchically superior to non-Western. Over time, international law emerged as a means to prevent and solve conflict and establish cooperation. And some of the main organizing elements are the economy and interdependence. Thus, the vision that emerged was different than that of the Islamic community (Krammer, 1991; Frankowski, 2010), African states (Murithi, 2023), and a more inward-looking Great China (Armstrong, 1994; Harding, 1993).

Still, there is a generally accepted vision among international relations scholars that the modern international system is an outgrowth of the Westphalian order. In this international understanding of the system, the normal unit of political and military action is the state, with its own defined borders and sovereignty. Therefore, the idea of nation-states was rooted in the 19th century and became the bases of the architecture of the Westphalian state system.

While this Westphalian order has undergone many changes since 1648, the essential elements of the system have survived, and state sovereignty is still one of the defining elements of the system. However, today there is also an increased perception that non-state actors have an important role in the development of international relations, and the system is become more fragmented and complex from the one that was established five centuries ago. This has been referred to as the post-Westphalian system.

The new world order

When a state has more power than any other actor in the international system, this will likely become the hegemonic power. This was the case of the United States after the Cold War. The Cambridge Dictionary (2024) defines this phase as the "new world order", "a political situation in which the countries of the world are no longer divided because of their support for either the US or the Soviet Union and instead work together to solve international problems". This interest for solving international problems comes from the liberal understanding on how states should prevent and deal with conflict, thus showing that the new world order became one based on international liberalism. In the words of Mearsheimer (2018):

> A state pursuing liberal hegemony aims to remake the international system in its own image. And this is what the United States did in the aftermath of the Cold War. It fostered an open world economy based on international trade, built international institutions, and promoted democratic values. These are the principles under which international liberalism is built, and which are believed to be the key to avoid interstate war. . . . States will see themselves as being part of an international community, and even citizens can feel as if being part of a world community.[1]
>
> (Mearsheimer, 2018)

As Gilpin (1846) puts it, "an international system is in a state of equilibrium if the more powerful states in the system are satisfied with the existing territorial, political, and economic arrangements". This rather realist vision of the international system assumes that the main struggles of states are still related to wealth and power. But what we have seen over time is that periods of transformation have been characterized by differing rates of change

1 To read more on the ideas of 'international community' and 'world community' see: Foreign Policy. (2002, September/October). What is the international community?; Leonard, M. (2002). Introduction: The contours of the world community. In M. Leonard (Ed.), *Re-ordering the world*. The Foreign Policy Centre; and Lindberg, T. (2014). Making sense of the "international community". *Council on Foreign Relations*, Working Paper. www.cfr.org/sites/default/files/pdf/2014/01/IIGG_WorkingPaper14_Lindberg.pdf

(Krishna-Hensel, 2010). The industrial, nuclear, and technology revolutions have all shaped new power relations between states and have mapped the world order as we know it to this day.

In the aftermath of Hiroshima and Nagasaki, the necessity for radical change in political thinking became evident. Traditional warfare was challenged by new technologies and had a potential of causing damage never seen before. The expansion of nuclear proliferation instigated a new urgency for conflict solution. But with continuing technological advancement, the acquisition of advanced up-to-date weaponry such as nuclear weapons, missiles, and drones has emerged "as a symbol of prestige and an indication of a nation's place in the hierarchy of international power" (Krishna-Hensel, 2010). Today there is a more intense element of uncertainty to the existing balance of powers that has characterized the international system for decades.

In the words of Krishna-Hensel (2010),

> the process of transformation and change of the international system has been an ongoing cumulative one. Many forces, including conflict, technological innovation, and communication have contributed to the creation of a trans-national world with political, economic, and social implications for all societies.

With the emergence of globalization, the world changed, and so have social relations with the advancement of new information and communication technologies. At the international arena, international relations have also taken new forms. Technological advancements can be a source of cooperation but also conflict between states, and they are also the basis for the increased prominence of the role of non-state actors in the international arena. Electronic communications, but also chemical and biotechnological developments, can empower non-state actors to levels never seen before, and even lead them to reach the status of becoming sources of new international security threats.

The collapse of the Soviet Union inaugurated a new order where not only states would be the main actors, but non-state actors would also be taking active roles. And contemporary threats undermining global peace and security now originate not only from states, but from non-state ones, as with the case of international criminal organizations. This new range of actors influenced the distribution of power and even the world order. And along with globalization, societies have evolved, and ideologies, economic and trade structures, and technological developments have shaped new social relations and international security threats.

It is then clear that today the sphere of dominance of security is no longer only at the hands of state actors, but also of new players. Globalization and the inclusion of non-state actors have led to the erosion of the concept of sovereignty,[2] a fundamental principle of the Westphalian order (Özlük & Çemrek, 2010). But the interference of non-state actors such as international terrorist organizations also shows the strong impact that their actions may have on international security, as seen in the 9/11 events.

The world order after 9/11

In the aftermath of the Second World War, the United States' military superiority was also backed up by a strong, dominant economy. The country had become a superpower. With the end of the Soviet Union, former communist states embraced economic freedom, and technological, transportation, and communication advancements were leading the world towards globalization.

However, this optimism did not last long, and with the arrival of the 21st century and the terrorist attacks of September 11, 2001, a series of events showed the fragile status of the liberal order and its main precursor. The United States failed to secure peace in its interventions in Iraq and Afghanistan, there was a financial crisis in 2008 that shook the global economy, and power seemed to be slowly shifting away from the United States after decades being at the forefront of political and economic life. At the national level, the populist upsurge within the US was first expressed by the Tea Party movement and later consolidated with the successful candidacy of Donald Trump. His policies focused on reinforcing national security and consistently argued that the US would only intervene in foreign affairs if this was in the interest of the nation and for its own security. Reinforcing borders, defense budget, and military powers were among his main objectives. To make this clear, the National Security Strategy of 2017 stated that the priority was to "protect American sovereignty", and that after promoting the liberal order "at the expense of the sovereignty of others", it would no longer be promoting the liberal international order (Trump, 2017).

Slowly but surely, nationalist parties began to emanate more evidently. Nationalism is a political ideology which focuses on nations. These are social units with distinct cultures, and they all aspire to have their own state. Thus, for nationalists, self-determination is key. An important difference – and source for problem – between nationalism and liberalism is their understanding of individual rights. While for the latter everyone has the same rights and all humans are equals, nationalism is only more concerned with the social unit and therefore prioritizes the rights of its fellow citizens. The nation is the

2 Özlük and Çemrek argue that this erosion of sovereignty brings the international system to a pre-Westphalian era, where there is a lack of political and social importance of borders. Different is the view of Krasner (1991, 2001), who argues that this transformation of sovereignty by globalization is an exaggerated discourse.

primary unit and citizens are its subordinates, bound by a common culture and identity, and a strong sense of loyalty.

Nations have been important for a long time in shaping cultures, traditions, ethnicities, religions, language, and, overall, a national identity. For many, the nation remains the largest unit with which one shares social attachment. But for decades now, human societies have grown larger, with globalization facilitating international communication and transportation, and thus breaking geographical barriers. Liberalism can be a positive vision for national identity as it can be a way to manage diversity in peaceful terms. However, interventions by Western nations in other countries have been perceived as an abuse of their power. While globalization and liberalism have provided many benefits, some have also felt their identities threatened by such universal patterns and by the values that are promoted behind national interests.

Western powers assumed that with the end of the Cold War, Russia would follow a natural progression to democracy. Over time, the expectations for the country were to follow the lines of its other post-Communist neighbors and converge to liberal values. Nevertheless, Russia has never left the hopes of being a superpower again and has looked at the West with disdain. It has continued constructing its narrative against non-Western identity, and today the country's main objective might be to become an independent pole in an increasingly multipolar global order (Mankoff, 2017). All the while, as the current order seems to be in crisis, non-Western multilateral blocs are emerging and being reinforced to counter Western power in the global arena. This way, groups like Brazil, Russia, India, China, and South Africa (BRICS) or the Shanghai Cooperation Organization (SCO) are seen as counterweights to liberal powers. Slowly but surely, they are gaining force, as the expansion of the BRICS shows with the addition of six new members to the forum in January 1, 2024 (Argentina, Egypt, Ethiopia, Iran, Saudi Arabia, and the United Arab Emirates).[3] As Moran (2021) puts it: "Apart from the apparent economic stagnation felt by many, the clarity of the Cold War era, when Americans knew who the enemy was, had also gone".

There was now no singular threat. There is now rising competition, more than just economic, between the United States and China. After years of progressively expanding its borders and threatening to respond to NATO's expansion, Russia has started an armed conflict against Ukraine. Israel is

3 For more information on their incorporation see: 'What to know about the 6 nations invited to join BRICS. *The New York Times*, 28 August. www.nytimes.com/2023/08/23/world/asia/brics-nations-new-members-expansion.html; Sumayya, I. (2023, August 24). A wall of BRICS': The significance of adding six new members to the bloc. *AlJazeera*. www.aljazeera.com/news/2023/8/24/analysis-wall-of-brics-the-significance-of-adding-six-new-members; Du Plessis, C., Miridzhanian, A., & Acharya, B. (2023, August 25). BRICS welcomes new members in push to reshuffle world order. *Reuters*. www.reuters.com/world/brics-poised-invite-new-members-join-bloc-sources-2023-08-24/

also fighting a war in Gaza. Iran has increasingly hegemonic ambitions in the Middle East Region. The European Union has seen the United Kingdom leave the Union after a decisive national referendum. But there are also other events and non-state actors shaping a chain of events leading to great change within the international order: the terrorist threat, cybercrime, the climate crisis. . . . The past years have led us to a "new geopolitical age" (Ramonet, 2022).

And this new age has arisen because of the many critiques towards the new world order. Globalization was perceived by some as a threat to regionalism, multiculturalism as a threat to national identities, and the West was seen as a dominant player making the rules in what it wanted to shape as its own system. The liberal order began being perceived by non-Western states as the American pursuit of global dominance (Anderson, 2002). And US military interventions are just but more proof that this is a hegemonic power seeking to maintain this status. As the 20th century came to an end, democracy was expanding, and the liberal international order seemed to have been successful in building a *new* world order. However, economic growth outside the US and Europe has shifted the balance and has dispersed economic power around the globe (Fox, 2012). And critiques against Western dominance have done nothing but keep growing. Furthermore, leaders like Viktor Orbán in Hungary, Jair Bolsonaro in Brazil, Recep Tayyip Erdoğan in Turkey, Javier Milei in Argentina, and Donald Trump in the United States have diminished liberal institutions. And across democratic states, populist, nationalist, and xenophobic discourses have spread.

Trump began his presidency with a commitment to focus on national security and made a series of unilateral decisions with enormous consequences. Many have questioned his actions to the point where he has even been blamed for undermining the international order. But he was not alone, and over time, nationalists have blamed liberals for breaking national community, cultural bonds, and identities. Liberalism has been blamed for spreading an anti-culture and dissolving nations, as it is a movement that is more concerned with global humanity than with fellow citizens (Deneen, 2018).

The effects of these changes

In early 2023, President Xi Jinping went to Moscow to visit President Vladimir Putin. During their farewells following talks, China's president told his Russian counterpart: "Right now there are changes – the likes of which we haven't seen for 100 years – and we are the ones driving these changes together". To which Putin responded, "I agree".[4]

4 To read more about the meeting in different media outlets see: Daalder, I. (2023, April 12). Xi is fixated on ending China's century of humiliation. *Politico*. Retrieved September 3, 2023, from www.politico.eu/article/xi-is-fixated-on-ending-chinas-century-of-humiliation/; Frachon, A. (2023, April 13). Russia and China are united in an ideological battle against the

Russia has been trying to expand its power – and even its borders – in the regions of Georgia, Crimea, and Western Ukraine, attempting to divide NATO and create chaos in the European Union. China is seen as a threat with both regional and global ambitions. The main aim of the United States, on the other hand, is to prevent the emergence of new centers of power that can challenge the American order. But Russia is a natural challenger of this order and of American power, and the strategies followed by Americans in the past years have vigorously generated rejection in the Kremlin. The United States has promoted the so-called Color Revolutions in Georgia in 2003 ("Rose Revolution"), Ukraine in 2004 ("Orange Revolution"), and Kyrgyzstan in 2005 ("Tulip Revolution"). These were non-violent protests aimed at establishing Western-like liberal democracies in these countries. But these neighboring countries to Russia are of great strategic importance to Moscow.

NATO's movement eastward has been seen by the Kremlin as a threat for a long time.[5] Since the end of the Cold War, Moscow has tolerated NATO's existence, but it has been opposed to its expansion. There was a first enlargement of its members in 1999 with Poland, Hungary, and the Czech Republic, but it continued growing over time. The real problem became evidently serious in 2008, when the addition of Ukraine and Georgia was officially presented at the table. Russia has since then made it clear that the membership of these countries in NATO would bring "serious consequences", as declared by the then Russian Deputy Foreign Minister (BBC, 2008).

Western officials contend that they have tried hard to relieve Russian uneasiness, but Ukraine is too strategically important to Russia to remain at the side and let the West increase the military alliance up to its borders. The Kremlin's response has finally been the use of force. And while observers of international politics believed that realism was a thing of the past, this has been proof that the world in which we are living is not entirely one where democratic values prevail, and that geopolitical calculations are still of great importance. In sum, there has been a clash between two different systems: the Russian, a realist one; and the Western, based on liberalism. And this clash has resulted in a major crisis with enormous consequences: a war.

West, and therefore against Europe. *Le Monde*. Retrieved September 3, 2023, from www.lemonde.fr/en/opinion/article/2023/04/13/russia-and-china-are-united-in-an-ideological-battle-against-the-west-and-therefore-against-europe_6022835_23.html and; Nanu, M. (2023, March 22). Watch: Xi Jinping tells Putin 'change not seen in 100 years' is coming. *The Telegraph*. Retrieved September 3, 2023, from www.telegraph.co.uk/world-news/2023/03/22/watch-xi-jinping-tells-putin-change-not-seen-100-years-coming/

5 For more on this discussion see: BBC News. (2014, September 3). Why Nato-Russia relations soured before Ukraine. *BBC News*. www.bbc.com/news/world-europe-29030744; International Crisis Group. (2014). Ukraine: Running out of time. Report 231. www.crisisgroup.org/europe-central-asia/eastern-europe/ukraine/ukraine-running-out-time; Masters, J. (2023). Ukraine: Conflict at the crossroads of Europe and Russia. *Council on Foreign Relations*. www.cfr.org/backgrounder/ukraine-conflict-crossroads-europe-and-russia

In the Chinese case, there is also resentment towards Americans and their continuous intents to promote human rights in the country, which are interpreted as a master plan to promote regime change. These moves to liberalize China have ultimately worsened relations between the two nations, and the United States is far from reaching its goal to democratize China. On the contrary, China believes that the architecture that was built by the West after World War II is becoming irrelevant and will undoubtedly lead to failure. Leonard (2023) brings a very suggestive perspective to understand the United States and China's vision of the decay of the world order through their interpretation of the war between Ukraine and Russia:

> The very different responses of China and the Unites States to Russia's invasion of Ukraine revealed the divergence in Beijing's and Washington's thinking. In Washington, the dominant view is that Russia's actions are a challenge to the rules-based order, which must be strengthened in response. In Beijing, the dominant opinion is that the conflict shows the world is entering a period of disorder, which countries will need to make steps to withstand.
>
> (Leonard, 2023)

Chinese efforts to create parallel international institutions and projects may be a sign of this view. The Asian Infrastructure Investment Bank (AIIB), the New Development Bank, and the Global Security Initiative (GSI) are all ways for Peking to mobilize itself and its position in world politics while becoming a key institutional player in shaping global security. For many years, China was seen as a growing economic power. Today, it is also a key player in international politics and a well-established diplomatic power, and it already has an important role in North Africa and the Middle East.

In the Middle East, the United States has also meddled in the governance of many countries and overruled leaders to implement democratic systems. These actions, which started strongly after the events of 9/11, have taken place in countries like Afghanistan, Iraq, Egypt, Libya, and Syria. In the cases of Afghanistan, Iraq, and Libya there was direct military intervention to promote regime change. In all of them, efforts have led to their failure and destruction, causing great civilian damage. China and other countries in the Global South have seen these interventions as an abuse of power by the United States. They share the vision that the West has abused the rules-based system it created for itself, applying norms selectively and changing them according to their national interests. It was therefore a matter of time that the liberal system failed because the same actors that built this order are the ones abusing it. And today there are actors actively pushing for the construction of a new international order.

This is precisely one of the things that the United States is afraid of: losing its hegemony to other powers trying to challenge it. It sees China and Russia as actors trying to reshape the balance of power in key regions of the world, both to become hegemons within their own spheres and thus change the features of the international order in their favor (Moran, 2021). However, many experts believe that China does not want to become the new hegemonic power, but it instead wants a multipolar world. In the words of Jeffrey Sachs, director of the Center for Sustainable Development at Columbia University, "China doesn't want the United States to be the preeminent power. It wants to live alongside the United States" (Goodman, 2023). In most regions, the most powerful state is the one defining its structure and relations, creating small poles of the system. Frankowski (2010) talks about an "archipelago called international order", consisting of different overlapping regional islets of order. This is an alternative view of what the coming world order may look like – a combination of different regional orders with different regional leaders. But the reality of these changes within the international order and what this will look like is yet to be seen.

Which order will prevail in the 21st century?

With the end of World War II, the United States and its allies had been building a world based on democratic values, open trade, cooperation in security matters, and multilateralism. International institutions were designed to support this system, and the United States was at the forefront as its leader. In November 1989 the Berlin Wall came down and in the two years that followed, borders opened, and the Soviet Union collapsed and dissolved into different republics. For many years, there had been a clash between different ideologies including communism, fascism, and liberalism. As the century came to an end, it seemed that liberalism had finally been successful in building a new world order. After the end of the Cold War, the levels of war and violence decreased. Even realists like Mearsheimer (2013) accepted that there had been less warfare since 1945, and especially since the end of the Cold War. These lower levels of violence worldwide were seen as a sign of the liberal triumph and the progress of liberal expectations. Twenty years after the end of the 20th century, liberalism was at its peak.

However, this optimism did not last long, and today this so-called liberal order is at an impasse. As Ikenberry (2020) explains, the two great powers that have helped build this system – the United States and Great Britain – now "seem to be pulling back from their leadership . . . [and] for the first time since 1945, the United States found itself led by a president who is actively hostile to the core ideas of liberal internationalism". China and Russia are the real dangers to a rules-based order and the biggest competitors to the hegemonic power of the United States. But they alone are not the only problem of the survival of the international order. There are problems with the foundations on which the regime was built, problems related to modernity. And this is precisely what non-Western states are now promoting: illiberal visions of civilization and modernity (Synder, 2018).

Perhaps China will fall into financial problems and live an overturn that will slow its growth and therefore exponential growth. If that is the case, the United States will not face great burdens to maintain its status as a hegemonic power. However, hegemonic powers can only maintain their position in a unipolar system. And if China continues growing the way it is predicted, a world based on a bipolar or multipolar structure is more likely to prevail. Therefore, the question here is whether the liberal or realist systems will be in charge of shaping this world order. Mearsheimer (2018) sustains that when great powers are confronted, they can only act according to realist dictates. Thus, according to him, even liberalism ends up devolving into realism in any system that is not unipolar. If this were the case, China and the United States would base their decisions to act within this system according to geopolitical calculations. The United States would probably continue following liberal principles, as this has long been part of its DNA. But both powers would try to prevent the other from becoming the new hegemon.

The United States thought that with the end of the Cold War and the prevalence of a liberal system, China and Russia would slowly but surely "listen to reason" and end up initiating a regime change, leave authoritarian institutions, and establish a political system closer to that of Western nations. This has not happened, and as recent events have shown, there is now a global turmoil that has left many international relations specialists wondering what the next era will look like. This is partly because Western states, in their belief that it is their responsibility to protect the human rights of all peoples, have intervened in other countries and not always with the main purpose to protect civilians' rights. Liberalism seeks to spread democracy by turning autocracies into liberal democratic states, interfering in the internal affairs of other countries and forging systems upon them. But this military intervention has been an imposition and has generated rejection by many non-Western states.

Since the Soviet Union fell, the reasons to intervene in a country have expanded. Western states first wanted to defend citizens of the world from human rights violations. When a state commits mass domestic violence, such as is the case with genocides or crime against humanity, there is general agreement that there is a need from the international community to protect peoples from such actions. However, the responsibility to protect cannot be used as a justification for great powers to intervene in weaker states. Over time, humanitarian reasons have increased and have even included intervention to protect from the terrorist threat and in the name of the Global War on Terror. And non-Western states are criticizing Western action as it is perceived to be merely covert actions to promote regime change and establish authorities in third countries which are favorable to the West.

Today the world order as we know it is in crisis. The unipolar era for which the post-Cold War was characterized has faded away and is now giving way to a new world order. China is rising as one of the biggest world powers, with foundations and values radically opposite to those of liberalism supported by the West. And Russia has resurged as another revisionist power also following illiberal ideologies. The importance of liberalism lies in its belief to promote and protect individual rights. And democratic states are the best to safeguard them. As Fukuyama (2022b) states, this might as well be the end of history in the sense that we have found no better alternative to liberal democracy.

Changes in the world order matter because orders are indispensable in the modern international system. From the one hand, they manage interstate relations in a highly independent world (Krasner, 1982; Keohane, 1984). International institutions and rules are the ones regulating these relations, making interactions more efficient and facilitating international cooperation to solve common concerns. Therefore, this interdependence is not only restricted to economic affairs, but it is also about addressing environmental, health, and security issues. Thus, international institutions such as the United Nations, North Atlantic Treaty Organization (NATO), the World Bank, and the International Monetary Fund (IMF) are just a few examples of institutions tackling this inter-state interaction. But these institutions, with the international legal system, also help manage the behavior of states and constrain their actions, making sure that the rules are obeyed. While it is true that this system of institutions and rules is shaped by powerful states and that these may be seen as "simply tools of the great powers" (Mearsheimer, 2019), these rules are still the essence of any institution and help manage relations between states. In sum, in an interconnected world such as the one we live in, a system of rules is necessary to lower transaction costs and help maintain a certain harmony within the international system.

Therefore, changes within the international order will also affect the international legal system. The ways in which norms are made, their content, and their use may change. In fact, we have already started seeing changes in these regards. And this is significantly important in a rules-based system such as the one we live in. These rules govern not only the obligations of states, but they also protect the rights of individuals. The next chapter will precisely explore these changes, how they may affect the international legal system, and their consequences.

Conclusion

This chapter has presented the different views of international relations studies while exposing current debates on whether and how the international order is being replaced by a new one. The events of the current century have triggered a series of power changes, including new rising powers, the rise of populist and nationalist discourses, and the spread of xenophobia and discrimination. Altogether, there seems to be a weakening of liberal institutions or even of democracy overall. This has led to the re-emergence of academic discussions on what this implies for the international order, wondering if we are facing the unfolding of a new order and, if so, what this will look like. The goal of this chapter was to present this theoretical framework and academic discussions in order to further understand what these changes may bring in the future, what this implies for the rules-based system and for international security. As will be seen in the following chapter, these alternations have also led to adjustments in the way states deal with international law. The following chapter intends to demonstrate that the way states respond to international security threats is changing. And instead of managing international concerns through multilateral cooperation and the establishment of common international norms, there has been a move towards dealing with external threats through domestic action, and thus prioritizing national security strategies and the development of national norms.

References

Acharya, A. (2007). The emerging regional architecture of world politics. *World Politics*, *59*(4), 629–652.

Anderson, P. (2002). Force and consent. *New Left Review*, *17*.

Armstrong, D. (1994). Chinese perspectives on the new world order. *The Journal of East Asian Affairs*, *8*(4), 454–481.

Barnett, M. (2021). International progress, international order, and the liberal international order. *The Chinese Journal of International Politics*, *14*(1), 1–22.

BBC. (2008, April 3). Nato denies Georgia and Ukraine. *BBC News*. Retrieved August 29, 2023, from http://news.bbc.co.uk/2/hi/europe/7328276.stm

Cambridge Dictionary. (2024). *The new world order*. Retrieved January 9, 2024, from https://dictionary.cambridge.org/es/diccionario/ingles/new-world-order

Carr, E. H. (1951). *The twenty-years crisis, 1919–1939: An introduction to the study of international relations*. Macmillan.

Deneen, P. J. (2018). *Why liberalism failed*. Yale University Press.

Fox, J. (2012). The new new world order. *Harvard Business Review*. Retrieved January 9, 2024, from https://hbr.org/2012/04/the-new-new-world-order

Frankowski, P. (2010). One world – many 'orders'?' In S. F. Krishna-Hensel (Ed.), *Order and disorder in the international system*. Ashgate Publishing.

Fukuyama, F. (2022a). *Liberalism and its discontents*. Profile Books.

Fukuyama, F. (2022b). More proof that this really is the end of history. *The Atlantic*. Retrieved August 30, 2023, from www.theatlantic.com/ideas/archive/2022/10/francis-fukuyama-still-end-history/671761/

Gilpin, R. (1846). *War and change in world politics*. Cambridge University Press.

Goodman, A. (2023, April 25). Jeffrey Sachs on China's "historic" push for multipolar world to end U.S. domination. *Democracy Now*. Retrieved September 4, 2023, from www.democracynow.org/2023/4/25/jeffrey_sachs_china

Harding, H. (1993). The concept of "Greater China": Themes, variations and reservations. *The China Quarterly*, *136*, 660–686.

Ikenberry, J. G. (2001). *After victory: Institutions, strategic restraint, and the rebuilding of order after major wars*. Princeton University Press.

Ikenberry, J. G. (2020). The end of liberal international order? *International Affairs*, *94*(1), 7–23.

Kant, I. (1991). Idea for a universal history with a cosmopolitan purpose. In H. Reiss (Ed.), *Kant's political writings*. Cambridge University Press. (Original work published 1795)

Keohane, R. O. (1984). *After hegemony: Cooperation and discord in the world political economy*. Princeton University Press.

Krammer, M. (1991). Islam in the new world order. In A. Ayalon (Ed.), *Middle east contemporary survey* (Vol. XV). Westview Press.

Krasner, S. D. (1982). International regimes. *International Organization*, *36*(2).

Krasner, S. D. (2001). Abiding sovereignty. *International Political Science Review*, *22*(3), 229–251.

Krishna-Hensel, S. F. (2010). *Order and disorder in the international system*. Ashgate Publishing.

Leonard, M. (2023, July/August). China is ready for a world of disorder. *Foreign Affairs*.

Mankoff, J. (2017). Russia's revival. In M. Dunn Cavelty & T. Balzacq (Eds.), *Routledge handbook of security studies*. Routledge.

Mazarr, M., Priebe, M., Radin, A., & Stuth Cevallos, A. (2016). Understanding the current international order. *RAND Corporation*. Retrieved March 8, 2024, from www.rand.org/content/dam/rand/pubs/research_reports/RR1500/RR1598/RAND_RR1598.pdf

Mearsheimer, J. J. (2013). Has violence declined in world politics? *Perspectives on Politics*, *11*(2), 570–573.

Mearsheimer, J. J. (2018). *The great delusion: Liberal drams and international realities*. Yale University Press.

Mearsheimer, J. J. (2019). Bound to fail: The rise and fall of the liberal international order. *International Security*, *43*(4), 7–50.

Molloy, S. (2021). Theorizing liberal orders in crisis then and now: Returning to Carr and Horkheimer. *International Studies Quarterly*, *65*(2), 320–330.

Moran, A. (2021). The US: Seeking security post-9/11. In P. Hough, A. Moran, B. Pilbeam, & W. Stokes (Eds.), *International security studies: Theory and practice*. Routledge.

Murithi, T. (2023, May/June). Order of oppression. Africa's quest for a new international system. *Foreign Affairs*.

Özlük, E., & Çemrek, M. (2010). Burying sovereignty in this birthplace: Back to the middle ages. In S. F. Krishna-Hensel (Ed.), *Order and disorder in the international system*. Ashgate Publishing.

Paine, T. (1992). *Rights of man* (G. Claeys, Ed.). Hackett Publishing. (Original work published 1791)

Ramonet, I. (2022, March 1). Una nueva edad geopolítica. *Le Monde Diplomatique en Español*. Retrieved August 28, 2023, from https://mondiplo.com/una-nueva-edad-geopolitica

Schweller, R. L. (2001). The problem of international order revisited. *International Security*, *26*(1), 161–185.

Synder, T. (2018). *The road to unfreedom: Russia, Europe, America*. Penguin.

Trump, D. J. (2017). *National Security Strategy of the United States of America (NSS)*. White House. Retrieved August 29, 2023, from https://trumpwhitehouse.archives.gov/wp-content/uploads/2017/12/NSS-Final-12-18-2017-0905.pdf

Waltz, K. N. (1979). *Theory of international politics*. Addison-Wesley.

2

The influence of international law in a new international order

The return to a Westphalian state system?

Theoretically, liberal democracies base their relations on multilateralism and cooperation. This is not only due to the economic gains that can be generated from international trade, but also because of the mutual goal to pursue international protection and security. This cooperation in the field of security has been aimed at preventing armed conflict and detering threats. And one way to do so has been through the construction of an international legal system with its own institutions.

A system of rules within the international order can be useful to avoid conflict and solve disputes. First, rules can facilitate international cooperation and, in general, any type of transaction. Second, rules also give information beforehand on the consequences of wrongful acts. They prevent cheaters from getting away with their transgressions. Their acts have consequences and can be punished, while those adhering to agreements are rewarded with trust and increased cooperation. Third, rules create a linkage between actors, which generates greater interdependence and in turn increases the costs of cheating. The rule of law has an important role in all these spheres, and an international body of norms is key to promote economic and social development, and to maintain international peace and security.

In international relations, the idea of sovereignty arose with the Treaties of Westphalia in 1648. Since then, states have been considered political units with the monopoly of force within their mutually recognized territories. They are all sovereign independent states within an international system. They have formal diplomatic ties and international law is the basis of these international relations. The domestic and international spheres remain separate, and one state cannot intervene in the internal affairs of another. At a smaller scale, sovereignty is also the power of an authority to control the decision-making process within a territory. And in today's modern democracies, this power rests in the citizens who, through electoral processes, select the leaders who will exercise this power through representative institutional bodies. Essentially, sovereignty can also be understood as the power to make laws.

DOI: 10.4324/9781003458159-3

With the end of the Cold War, there was a common understanding that governments were expected to protect the human rights of individuals and that failure to protect them could cause legitimate concern of other international actors and the international community. According to this vision, states were no longer responsible for protecting their territories and their citizens, but there was also a duty to protect the human rights of those residing in other nations where the state failed to do so. A "post-Westphalian" system emerged, one where international authority structures and supranational interests prevailed (Kreuder-Sonnen & Zangl, 2015).

Nevertheless, in recent years we have seen an increase in conflict, but also of impunity (Colomina et al., 2023). There even seems to be a comeback of territorial disputes. While it seemed that in this century we had long left behind these types of controversies, conflicts to gain territorial control have proliferated, as the conflicts in Ukraine, Gaza, and Nagorno-Karabakh have recently shown. There seems to be a return of an order based on geopolitics. But the idea of what "geopolitics" means has varied since its beginnings.

The notion is best known to have been used since the origins of the nation-state as an international actor after the Peace of Westphalia in 1648, which put an end to the Thirty Years' War in Europe. One of the first theorists in the discipline was Friedrich Ratzel, who used the idea of the "Kampf um Raum" (Fight for Space) in the book "Political Geography" of 1897. His geopolitical theory was focused on the relationship between geography and the political system, as he believed that the expansion of a state's territory was associated with the expansion of its economy, politics, development, and, altogether, influence. For him, space was vital for geopolitics, and he suggested that it was key for a state to govern certain spaces (land) and its resources to secure its survival (Costachie & Damian, 2010; Hernández, 2022). Later, theorists like Alfred Thayer Mahan, Halford MacKinder, and Henry Kissinger contributed to the nature of the concept of geopolitics with diverse perspectives, theories, and elements.

History then shows that theories evolve, and so has the concept of geopolitics. While at its core it remains a combination of geography and politics, understanding that power politics are influenced by geographical factors, these factors have widely varied over time. In the current international scenario, geopolitics is no longer only the expansion of land or sea, or the balance of political constellations. It has new elements that are equally important. The rise of disruptive technologies such as artificial intelligence or quantum computers will also shape how great powers use them for geopolitical gains, as the advantage they provide will also be a key factor for achieving superiority in confrontation. Cybersecurity has also become part of the arsenal in times of conflict, as attacks in the cybersphere are highly sophisticated, are persistent, and can lead to crucial infrastructure damage for the opponent. In sum, today geopolitics are not only based on purely territorial gains, but are also conditioned by the economy, technology, and the cyber sphere, among other factors.

Therefore, the image that we had immediately built after the end of the Cold War and the one we are facing today are quite different. Back then, there was good reason to think that wars were becoming obsolete, that conflicts over territory were disappearing, and that violence was vanishing from the international system. Between 1992 and 2005, violent conflicts fell by some 40% (Mack, 2007). In the 1990s many civil wars ended, such as those in Cambodia, Lebanon, and Mozambique, as these were no longer useful as fields of influence between the Soviet Union and the West (Lacina, 2004). The level of economic interdependence across the world was growing at a rate we had not seen before. Democratization was taking place.

As put by Salamé (SIPA, 2022), "In the very first years of this Century, the three major vehicles for the optimism of the liberal order came to a halt, almost at the same time". The elements he sets for are democratization, economic interdependence, and globalization. While democracy reached a peak at the end of the 1990s, it then started to "stagnate" (SIPA, 2022). New countries were not becoming democratic, and some democratic ones faced *coup d'états* (i.e. Myanmar, Thailand, and Burkina Faso). On top of that, the quality of democracy was dropping.

As stated by Freedom House, "For years now, authoritarians have been on the offensive, while liberal democratic practices have increasingly been discarded" (Smeltzer & Buyon, 2022). The numbers are unequivocal:

> The present threat to democracy is the product of 16 consecutive years of decline in global freedom. A total of 60 countries suffered declines over the past year, while only 25 improved. As of today, some 38 percent of the global population live in Not Free countries, the highest proportion since 1997. Only about 20 percent now live in Free countries.
>
> (Repucci & Slipowitz, 2022)

The Democracy Index led by The Economist shows similar numbers, revealing that only 8% of the world's population lived in full democratic countries in 2022 (The Economist, 2023). The International Institute for Democracy and Electoral Assistance concluded in 2022 that half of the world's democracies were in retreat, and that between 2016 and 2021, the number of countries moving towards authoritarian regimes had more than doubled (IDEA, 2022).

In democratic states, violent events have materialized after free democratic elections. Rioters in the Capitol of the United States in 2021 to overturn the results of the presidential elections in the country are an example of the same illiberal forces that are corrupting democratic institutions. Hundreds of sympathizers of Jair Bolsonario irrupted in the Congress of Brazil after Lula da Silva took office in 2023. These events are just but another example that change is happening, and that liberal democracies must be reinforced if we want them to endure. Repucci and Slipowitz (2022), from Freedom House, summarize the changes within the international order over the past 20 years:

> For much of the 21st century, however, democracy's opponents have labored persistently to dismantle this international order and the restraints it imposed on their ambitions. The fruits of their exertions are now apparent. The leaders of China, Russia, and other dictatorships have succeeded in shifting global incentives, jeopardizing the consensus that democracy is the only viable path to prosperity and security, while encouraging more authoritarian approaches to governance.
>
> (Repucci & Slipowitz, 2022)

While these changes had been baking for a while against the abuse of the West, the events of September 11 set a landmark, and a new wave of securitization began. Securitization then becomes another sign of this changing international order. Since 2001, there has been an apparent return by states to recenter their focus on the units of the territory and the population (Foot, 2005), and different domains have been securitized. Securitization theory shows that certain political issues can be presented as security threats that need to be dealt with certain urgency because of the danger they pose to the nation or society. It also asserts that "issues are not essentially threatening in themselves; rather, it is by referring to them as 'security' issues that they become security problems" (Eroukhmanoff, 2018). Buzan et al. (1998), when introducing the notion of securitization, referred to the military, environmental, economic, societal, and political sectors. For instance, in the name of protecting national security, counter-terrorist legislation has diminished some of the rights of the population. And over time, discourses connecting the terrorist threat with immigration have expanded. While securitization theory can be analyzed from different issue areas, the field of migration will also be the one concerning the central question of this book.

In sum, what securitization shows in the context of international relations is that national security and the protection of sovereignty remain the most important units for the state, and that liberal values seem to be sidelined when confronted with security matters. The European Union, a strong advocate of the liberal order, has also moved towards these securitization practices in the field of migration. Since the beginning of the century, the EU has prioritized security issues to facilitate the use of short-term policymaking instead of political or economic reforms, which would require long-term policies. This is the case, for instance, of EU-Maghreb countries relations. As Joffé (2008) argues, in the aftermath of 9/11, these relations became based mostly on the securitization of migration and on controlling transnational terrorism, instead of the normative objectives that used to characterize the objectives of the EU in the Maghreb area. There has been what he called an "externalization-in-reverse", as this prioritization for security issues has nullified the normative policies that the EU had previously adopted in the area. He poses a series of questions and concerns on the implications that these actions may have for the EU:

> This pattern of events raises other questions as well, not least as to the real novelty of the Union's normative agenda and of the degree to which it really wishes to act as a normative power. It may well seek to project its values but to what extent can those values be described as universal and to what extent are they merely a projection of a specifically European agenda? It also revives the argument as to whether the European Union is really – as it now claims – an experiment in supranationalism or whether it is still trapped within the intergovernmental arena.
>
> (Joffé, 2008)

As a result of Russia's 2022 invasion of Ukraine, there was an important shift by some states in Europe. Firstly, Denmark changed its almost 30-year opt-out direction regarding EU security and defense matters, and in June 2022 the Danes decided to abandon this reservation and join EU and security defense. Secondly, Finland and Sweden also gave up their long-term neutrality and applied to join NATO in May of the same year. Thirdly, Germany passed a constitutional amendment to provide additional budget to their armed forces and renew its army equipment. While this may seem unimportant, if one analyzes defense issues within the country, it can be seen that these have been rather neglected by German politicians, thus increasing the budget for armed forces now represents an important "paradigm shift" (Moser, 2022).

National security has gained relevance through liberal states, and while the West used to be the promoter of universal values, it has slowly shifted its security policies towards protecting the nation from external threats. Trump made this move evident during his presidency, but the European Union has also seen its states increase military budgets and strengthen border control. The securitization of migration is just but another example of these measures moving states away from liberalism and bringing them back to centering their agendas through the lens of security and the protection of the nation.

International law-making in the 21st century

We are well aware of some of today's armed conflicts in Ukraine and Gaza. But there are also other conflict zones determining the future of the world's order. I am referring to those in the South China Sea and the Arctic region. The return for geostrategic considerations and realist calculations by big powers, the emphasis on power sources, and the return of international realist conceptions show a system in constant competition (García et al., 2019).

International commitments are also backsliding. The last significant multilateral agreement was the 2015 Paris Agreement on climate change (Sending, 2022).

The United Nations Climate Change Conference of 2023 (COP28) in Dubai was the first event of the kind to produce a text that explicitly recognized the need for "transitioning away from fossil fuels" (oil, coal, and gas) as a response to the climate crisis (UNSDG, 2023). Paradoxically, at the same time, the International Energy Agency (IEA) expects that global demand for oil, coal, and natural gas will reach its peak this decade, based only on current policy settings (IEA, 2023). WTO members can invoke exceptions, but only in exceptional circumstances, as there must be a balance between states' interests and their obligations to reduce barriers to trade. Nevertheless, trade restrictions on national security grounds have proliferated in recent years, as well as questions on the connection between trade and national security (Bacchus, 2022). Multilateralism as a system of rulemaking seems to be in decline. Firstly, because very little is happening, with few international agreements being concluded. Secondly, because even when agreements are reached – being mostly declarations or soft mechanisms without binding obligations – the content of the same texts is often overlooked. In a way, the war in Ukraine is seen as an existential threat, not only for the country at stake, but for the principles of the rules-based order (Sending, 2022). On a similar note, Nigerian President Muhammadu Buhari made a statement at the UN General Assembly in September 2022, on the effects of the armed conflict in Ukraine:

> Such a conflict will have adverse consequences for us all, hindering our capacity to work together to resolve conflicts elsewhere, especially in Africa, the Middle-East and Asia. Indeed, the ongoing war in Ukraine is making it more difficult to tackle the perennial issues that feature each year in the deliberations of this Assembly, such as nuclear disarmament, the right of the Rohingya refugees to return to their homes in Myanmar, and the Palestinians' legitimate aspirations for statehood and reduction of inequalities within and amongst nations.
>
> (Buhari, 2022)

Even in the case of the United States, the hegemonic power that endured the international order, we see a decline in multilateralism and advancement of international treaty law. Trump took office being clearly hostile towards international treaties. Following his ideals of "America first", he even withdrew the country from the United Nations Human Rights Council (AJIL, 2018). But this decline in treaty law was also seen by his predecessor, Barack Obama, as he submitted far fewer treaties to the Senate for approval than previous presidents (Peake, 2018).

As put by Salamé, there has been a "deregulation of force" (Bobin, 2022). Colomina argues that the capacity to govern of international law has been diminished, and an example of this lack of enforcement is precisely the dispute between Prime Minister Benjamin Netanyahu of Israel and

Secretary-General António Guterres on the legitimacy and influencing role of the United Nations on the Israel-Palestine conflict (Barcos, 2024). And while international events are becoming more unpredictable, there is also an erosion of international norms (Colimina, 2023). Sending (2022) describes this decay of multilateralism:

> The multilateral system will be further undermined, that new efforts at multilateral rule making will be blocked, and that multilateralism will be used more and more as a tool to be exploited rather than a framework for international cooperation. This does not mean that there will not be multilateral governance, in the form of loans from the IMF, development finance available from the World Bank, and operational work by UN agencies on a range of issues. But it does mean that we will see more club governance, increased reliance on private actors and funding, and more fragmentation with great powers advancing competing agendas through these organizations. This is happening at a time when the need for stability in international rules, and beefed up governance capacity to prevent and manage global challenges is greater than ever.
>
> (Sending, 2022)

Jorgensen (2020) explores the rule of law through the lens of American foreign policy. In his book, he analyzes five different competing conceptions of the international rule of law through the lens of American foreign policy ideology: legalism, liberal internationalism, illiberal internationalism, liberal nationalism, and illiberal nationalism. At this point, it is particularly insightful to compare the notions of liberal and illiberal internationalism. Liberal internationalism is one of the ideal American policy types. This identifies the rule of law "in externalization of American constitutional government to establish a seamless system of law" (Jorgensen, 2020), with both national and international legal systems supporting liberal values, and where democracy is then a constitutive of the international rule of law. What the rule of law should achieve in this sense is a steady progression for greater freedom and conscience (Slaughter, 2007). Illiberal internationalism, on the other hand, uses the international legal system to clear the way for American foreign policy objectives. As put by Jorgensen (2020),

> The rule of law for illiberal internationalists means a flexible framework of legal rules and institutions that facilitates US strategic autonomy and diplomatic justifications. . . . International law is thereby preserved as a diplomatic tool between states rather than a means for vindicating the legal rights of natural persons.

The views of liberal and illiberal internationalism from a US foreign policy perspective exemplify the same contradictions that some states face when looking at the world order and the international legal system under which it stands. The liberal order seeks to promote liberal values, those connected to democracy, international trade, individual rights, and human dignity. But it has also been abused by the same hegemonic power that established it, intervening in the domestic affairs of less powerful states and being used to advance its own national interests. What stands out about the comparison between all five competing conceptions of the rule of law in the context of American foreign policy is that they all integrate a "strategic formulation for advancing [American national interests] through law" (Jorgensen, 2020).

Krisch (2005) discerns this use and misuse of international law, arguing that it can serve both as an instrument to exercise dominance and as an element of resistance to it. From the one hand, international law bows to the demands of powerful states in order not to be entirely sidelined. On the other hand, if it serves the powerful only, it may appear as a mere tool, unable to provide the legitimacy they seek. As explained in the previous chapter, some states have seen the international legal system, and the international order, as one reflecting only the values and interests of a dominant West. And as a response, states like China and Russia, but also others such as those being part of the BRICS or the Middle East, are today contesting this Western hegemony and calling for an order that also represents them. In this context, international law should not be seen as undesirable, but as a tool that provides legitimacy, humanitarianism, and "order".

Securitization processes such as those seen in the field of migration are another sign that the order as we know it is changing. Again, these practices are another example of the ways through which states prioritize adopting national legislation and policies to address what they see as international "security threats". In turn, this serves as an additional example of this return to national security and bringing at the forefront of the security arena the protection of national sovereignty. International concerns such as those in relation to migration, terrorism, climate change, and others are thus not addressed through the lens of multilateralism and international law. They are instead managed mostly domestically, even when they have a clear international reach. Sovereignty remains the most important unit for the state, and today it seems to be moving away from the liberal values that had been established in the past decades. Thus, while with the end of the Cold War it seemed that the protection of human rights and the promotion of liberal values would be at the center of the international arena, national political interests are regaining prominence in today's political affairs, if they ever lost it.

Vietti and Scribner (2013) argue that from a sovereignty perspective, irregular migration is perceived as an attack on the state's sovereignty, which justifies the deployment of immigration officers and frontier guards, as well as the construction of border fences. The worsening image of refugees given by some governments and media outlets presents them as invaders from which we need to protect. The systematic representation of the image of refugees as threats to our security has put them at the forefront of many national security agendas and has led to a rise of populist and extremist parties. As argued by Massimino (2017), the increasing number of ultra-right nationalist groups and their supporters in Europe poses an existential threat to European democracies and to the European Union.

Recent practices securitizing migration have shown that there is a preference for national security over human security. National self-interests and the protection of national territory come first, even before the security of vulnerable groups such as that of migrants. What the securitization of migration shows in this respect is that the new geopolitical model and a potential return of a more realist vision of politics strongly affects the rights of unprotected or more exposed groups. As a result of these changes within the international order, states prioritize national security and defence strategies over the protection of the rights of vulnerable groups of persons.

The effects of prioritizing national interests and national norm-development over international norm emergence, leads to creating new patterns around the globe and for more states to adopt the same strategy in a kind of spill-over effect. This was what happened after 9/11, when the United States reacted adopting hard security norms restricting the rights of immigrants in the country. This is a practice which has been reinforced thereafter not only in the United States, but also abroad. Ever since, there has been a new wave of securitization practices, and securitization laws and policies in the field of migration have become rather common in regions around the world, as explored in Chapters 5 to 8. When new security measures are adopted in a group of countries or in a region, this can easily lead to other states following with similar behaviors. When these states already face immigration concerns, this serves as an impulse to further justify the adoption of national security controls. And this has been the case with migration, an area which has become highly securitized.

If we consider law development as a flexible process in which different actors participate, we also see a change in the way international law has been promoted in the past years. As will be discussed in the following section, states are not the only actors interested in securitizing migration. It is not a matter of states alone or of international organizations, but civil society and private actors have a huge impact in the design of new norms. And actors such as Private Military and Security Companies (PMSCs) are today highly involved. Some scholars (Kaunert & Ezeokafor, 2022; Mabon, 2018) have already emphasized the role of non-state actors in the securitization process, thus showing the importance of a wide range of actors intervening in the construction of security threats. This book will also refer to the influence of private actors in the decision-making process and in securitization practices, although the main focus will remain at the state level.

Actors such as PMSCs have an important role in shaping norms and policies in the security arena, as the interplay between government and private entities has become key in today's norm-making processes. In the field of migration, there has been a privatization of the sector, as these companies do not merely provide border security and control services or consultant advice to governments, but they actively frame, shape, and implant militarized responses. Governments and regional bodies have shifted the burden to deal with forced migration towards non-state actors to "blur" their responsibility with refugees. Their responses to deal with these migratory flows have been directed to the security sphere, with an increased and more technical control of the borders, the militarization of the way we deal with migratory-related issues, and a decrease of the protection of human rights (Morgades, 2017, p. 38).

Furthermore, new ways of understanding the international legal system have also evolved, from voices claiming a growing relevance of Soft Law, to those defending a new doctrine of sources, to theories of new forms of creating norms such as informal law-making. Altogether, this has meant that a new way to understand international law and the international system has emerged, partly due to the continuous changes that the international order is facing, and partly due to the impact of globalization, which has led to a continuous renovation of the way international norms are made. A change in the way we recognize and accept law has mutated since the traditional doctrine of sources of international law.

This change of direction of international law, when mixed together with the changes within the global order and power forces, shows a completely new picture for the future of the international legal system. The Brexit in the European Union; Trump's unilateralist vision during his presidency in the United States; security issues like the climate crisis, terrorist attacks, and nuclear threats, are just a few examples of the events which have shaped the 21st century. And more recently, the invasion of Ukraine by Russia of 2022, or the escalation of the Israeli-Palestine conflict in 2023 bring us back to old military conflicts. All these episodes are crystallizing the era of change that we are living in, where geopolitical interests and national security come first, and international cooperation and problem-solving are somehow sidelined. This does not mean that the international legal system fails to be observed, but it does raise awareness on the maintenance of international peace and security as some thought it would be after the end of the Cold War. And today it is becoming more important than ever to secure the prevalence of the protection of human rights above all.

We seem to have forgotten that it is not only important to protect the security of the nation (national security), but we also need to secure that of the individual (human security). According to the 1994 UNDP report, human security is both "freedom from fear" (i.e. threats from war or violence) and "freedom from want" (i.e. poverty, pandemics, etc.). In this report, the UN agency enumerates seven different categories which can lead to human security threats: economic, food, health, environmental, personal, community, and political (UNDP, 1994). Failure to protect the individual from one or more of these categories can lead to increasing the vulnerability of already ill-protected groups such as refugees. Economic crises, environmental disasters, and political, religious, or ethnic persecution, can all lead to forcing families to leave their homes in search for a safe haven. Internally displaced peoples and refugees are a result of these and other catastrophic events, thus migration results from and can lead to human insecurity.

Thence if we continue focusing on the national security perspective instead of the human security one, we are opening the pathway to militarizing migration, that is, increasing surveillance and border control and allowing the detention and deportation of immigrants. In sum, more restrictive security policies and a more restrictive legal framework. And contrary to what some appear to believe, establishing prohibitions and restrictions to migration will not increase the security of the state, but will mostly diminish the security of these already vulnerable groups.

New age, new threats

Global governance is compounded by rules and systems of rules that result in a rule-governed behavior at the global level. While international norms used to be designed and addressed to deal with the relationship between states, global governance arrangements today involve a wide range of actors, including public and private actors, from private companies to the citizenry.

Globalization, privatization, and the fragmentation of states have introduced new actors in the international legal sphere (Creutz et al., 2019). International law's subjects and scope have varied over time, and past definitions – such as those referring to international law as "the law of nations" whose rules only applied to states – have become old-fashioned and in misuse, since the literature has shown that this definition and its scope has changed (Whytock, 2016). Thus, focusing solely on states as actors of international law could provide a misleading picture of international law-making (Boyle & Chinkin, 2007).

While debates on world legislation date back to the 20th century (Wessel, 2011), in the past years, discussions on the role of international actors in the international law-making process have expanded, and there seems to be some agreement on the idea that "law-making is no longer the exclusive preserve of states" (Boyle & Chinkin, 2007). Much of the power that non-state actors have in shaping international legislation and legal measures is influential, as they have specific knowledge in particular areas and thus can help in the shaping of new standards and operations with their expertise. International organizations, NGOs, and civil society organizations are some examples of actors contributing to making international law.

But there are also other actors such as transnational enterprises or multinational corporations, seeking to expand their business interests across countries. This does not necessarily mean that their interests represent those of the state. While they became more manifested during the 1950s and 1960s, they have become more powerful over time. Throughout the years, the idea that there are different types of international subjects besides states has gained momentum, and sovereignty does not seem to be the determinant feature that defines an international actor anymore (Ibáñez, 2016). Instead, characteristics like autonomy, influence, and the willingness to participate in international affairs have become increasingly important (Pareja-Alcaraz, 2010).

The role of non-state actors has been addressed in the field of international law-making, but it is also important in shaping international events that lead to new power structures or geopolitical concerns. The 9/11 bombings became the first attack ever to be directed against the United States by a non-state actor. This raised questions even for realists, who had centered states as the main and sole unit of the international system (Buzan & Hansen, 2009). Now an actor they had not perceived to be as relevant as the state was precisely the one to attack a country and shake the international security panorama.

McFate (2015) comments that this multiplicity of actors has led states to lose their centrality in the international order. For instance, software multinationals and their support to a specific software program can affect public spending (Wright, 2020). When a private company owning the keys to 5G is regarded as a threat to national security, the refusal to purchase its equipment delays the adoption of 5G coverage and, consequently, also the modernization of certain areas (Monti, 2020). In the words of Monti and Wacks (2022), "the decline of governmental power has increasingly placed the reins of public sector in the hands of private, supranational entities that control every aspect of our Matrix-like existence".

The involvement of PMSCs is evident in the field of security as they are shaping the legal and policy measures implemented in a wide range of countries. PMSCs are participating in armed conflicts such as that between Russia and Ukraine, but they are also actively involved in the regular administration of security services of states. They are controlling territorial borders, and, in the case of migration, they are also involved in deportations, detention, housing, and transportation. And they are not only providing these services to states but are also actively involved in the framing and shaping of them (Davitti, 2019). Through their lobbying and involvement in regulatory processes, it is hard to separate their interests from those of the international community when they are at the negotiating table. The more influence they have, the higher their economic profit, and they have created a security market with new technologies, which states heavily rely and depend on. As a result, there has been a normalization of the use of PMSCs in the context of migration. The increasing need to provide security services and improve technologies has paved the way for these companies to expand throughout and reinforce their role as the security guarantor. Today, "these measures have become everyday policies integrated in our societies and which many believe to be necessary for the normal functioning of the state" (Planas, 2023).

In the field of migration and security, they are heavily involved in the draft and negotiation process of security measures and strategies. And with their participation, they are "helping to classifying irregular migration as a security threat and framing the situation as a 'crisis', one that can only be addressed through emergency responses" (Planas, 2023). As explained in a report by Statewatch and the Transnational Institute,

> the EU is always keen to proclaim its origins in and ongoing commitment to upholding peace, human rights, democracy, and the rule of law, and promoting diplomacy and soft power over militarism and war. Upon closer examination, however, the bloc's spending priorities make clear that its identity as a political project is shifting.
>
> (Jones et al., 2022)

And this shift towards prioritizing national security has occurred in the past years and has intensified over time. National security has always been used as a reason to justify a wide range of political decisions. However, there are different scenarios, and some may seem more easily justifiable than others. We have recently gone through a pandemic where the restriction of rights was unquestioned because of the alarming consequences and uniqueness of the situation. A different situation was that in relation to the Global War on Terror, where the army and law enforcement powers were used to respond to the 9/11 events.

Global governance is highly concerned with security threats. But one needs to keep in mind that national security threats evolve over time and are also used according to different ideas. Ullman offered a definition of national security threat a few decades ago that did not include terrorism (1983):

> A threat to national security is an action or sequence of events that (1) threatens drastically and over a relatively brief span of time to degrade the quality of life for the inhabitants of a state, or (2) threatens significantly to narrow the range of policy choices available to the government of a state or to private, nongovernmental entities (persons, groups, corporations) within the state.
>
> (Ullman, 1983)

However, this is a rather old definition, and more recently other authors have identified a national security threat as any action or event conducive of negative consequences for the state or society (Krahmann, 2005). Therefore, there are new threats today and these seem to have a much wider range. Bello (2017) refers to these new threats in the following words:

> The particular novelty of *new threats* consists of the unpredictable extension that they can reach; in fact, new threats are characterized by

> unpredictability in terms of 1) occurrence, 2) places and agents involved, and 3) duration. They implicate perceptions of insecurity that concerns an extended number of states perceiving common menaces.
>
> (Bello, 2017)

Furthermore, it is also important to note that there is a subjective element, as threats are also shaped by the actors' perceptions and/or misperceptions (Duelfer & Dyson, 2011). Threats have an important psychological element, and our perception of what a threat is and is not can change over time, or according to what is presented to us as a potential danger.

In fact, in the case of migration, this increase in border policies and border control has not stopped or lowered the number of migrants trying to reach these shores (Avdan, 2012). Instead, it has increased the market for irregular crossings (Dunn, 2009; Bello, 2017). And negative public perceptions have also contributed to further securitizing migration. With inflation, debts, and economic crisis, sectors such as public health or education have been affected by cuts in recent years. As a result, citizens were faced with more unstable lives, and were concerned about maintaining their jobs and providing for their families. And when a period of economic instability is mixed with a salient number of incoming migrations, the perception of migrants as threats to the security of ordinary people is intensified, discourses linking migration to security are more easily believed, and prejudices are spread throughout.

These factors are then also used in public debates by certain groups to justify the need to stop immigrant flows into their countries or regions. While the unstoppable growing number of refugees has also raised awareness of their vulnerable situations and has turned into support by many, others have also felt threatened by their presence and have started proliferating discourses advocating for greater controls of migrant flows. The political elite, supported by the media, have presented refugee flows as a crisis, and a feeling of insecurity has been spread throughout.

Furthermore, terrorist attacks have exacerbated these perceptions and have reinforced the connection between migration and security. The attacks against the Twin Towers and the Pentagon in 9/11 were just the first of many terrorist attacks in Western countries, the aftermath of which has always witnessed discussions on whether refugee waves hide potential terrorists and debates questioning the reception and integration of immigration. As a result, many have started looking at migrants not just as an economic threat, but as a security threat.

In sum, the century has brought a series of changes that, when put together, have shaken the international security scenario. States are not the only actors perpetrating attacks and threatening international security, but they are also not alone in the law-making process. Instead, other actors such as private companies are also actively participating in legislating and negotiating policies, deciding security strategies, and framing new security threats. In the case of migration, the events of 9/11 were just the first of a series of terrorist attacks which have continuously presented immigrant communities as a source for concern. And after times of economic recession such as the 2008 financial crisis, or of instability such as with the migration crisis of 2015, the idea of an immigrant as a security threat has been reinforced. And over time, the image of the migrant as a dangerous outsider has been entrenched. Thus, when all of these elements are mixed, the result is an increasing and unstoppable process of securitization of migration which has been extended to this day. There are political actors interested in regaining control over certain areas, private actors with interests in securitizing them, and a changing global order that has even re-shaped the ways in which the law is made. States are returning to prioritizing national security, and migrants are the ones to pay the consequences.

Security at the border

Border control is a fundamental part of states' sovereignty. States are the ones to decide who is allowed to enter their territories and under what conditions. Border control has also become a typical securitization element in the field of migration. As such, a question that arises is in relation to state sovereignty and migration: What are the reasons to expel a foreigner and how is this linked to state sovereignty? As explained by Guild (2009), there are three main reasons, and they are all connected to security. Firstly, and most simply, states may expel a migrant if they are in the territory of the state illegally. This can be due to not having authorized the entrance of the individual, or because the individual has overstayed his or her permission. This breach is in relation to the power of the state to control who is in its territory and the more a state invests in border controls, "the higher the stakes against the foreigner who has not fulfilled the conditions" (Guild, 2009). The individual is categorized as "illegal", and this illegality in itself is a security issue (Bogusz et al., 2004). A second main reason to expel a migrant is because he or she has committed a criminal act. In this case, the foreigner is within the territory of a state lawfully but is expelled because he or she has breached national criminal laws. The third common ground is in relation to national security, meaning that the individual is a threat to the security of the nation, and collective security is prioritized. The century has come with discourses presenting immigrants, including refugees and asylum seekers, as security threats and even as potential terrorists. In the United States, asylum seekers have been conceptualized in the context of terrorism, assuming that they penetrate the country through asylum systems to then perpetrating attacks (Baylis, 2008). The term "immigrant" has come to be associated with a pejorative meaning, associated with "suspect" and "potential hostile foreigner" (Bigo, 2008). Gibney (2004) contends, "Many of these connections are greatly exaggerated: a tribute to the enduring force of stereotypes and the vulnerability of new entrants rather than a victory for objective data". And states have been unwilling to provide protection to these groups in the name of national security. In the words of Guild (2009):

> The framing of the security issue as one of balance, between the duty of the state to ensure public and national security and the right of the individual to protection against return to a country where he or she fears torture, leads away from the protection needs of the individual. The argument always privileges the state position as it is inherently state-centred: the state's duty to its people by definition excludes the refugee seeking protection. As the purpose of the state is to serve its people, the refugee is constructed as the outsider whose claims can be sacrificed in the name of the collective.
>
> (Guild, 2009)

The idea that has remained since September 11 is to securitize migration, refrain unwanted immigrants from coming, and depict them as an external threat. Walia (2021) identifies four main border governance strategies. The first one is based on exclusion, based on expelling unwanted migration by using walls, detention centers, and deportations. Restrictions to enter and remain in the country are designed and migrants are *made* illegal. There is an association between unwanted migration and its criminalization. The second strategy is territorial diffusion through the internalization and externalization of border control. The state thus monitors and restrains migrants within its territory, but also beyond its borders. These restrictions within the state can be measures to limit access to services that citizens enjoy such as healthcare, childcare, education, voting, etc. Externalization measures refer to interdictions of boats at sea, offshore detention, readmission agreements with third countries, safe third country agreements, among other examples. A third strategy of border governance is the commodification of migrants with deflated labor power to guarantee capital accumulation. Since these migrants risk deportation, they are diverted towards labor exploitation. A final strategy occurs through the discourses used by the political elite and the media to refer to migration. Immigration is often connected to higher crime rates, and refugees (and the so-called refugee crisis) are presented as a threat to the welfare system. Altogether, these measures put barriers to the enjoyment of basic rights of migrants while also complicating their integration into the host society.

However, as states and other actors continue drawing a picture of the migrant as an external threat from which society and the nation need protection, there is an important number of migrants, including refugees, fleeing from conflict, devastation, and poverty with the only intent to improve their lives and that of their families. Gibney (2004) challenges two assumptions that, he argues, people make about states and refugees. The first of these assumptions refers to the West and the creation of refugees. He argues that it is often assumed that liberal democratic states have few or no duties towards refugees, since they are not the ones responsible for their fleeing their country of origin. These states are the ones to blame, since they are the ones persecuting based on discrimination against them based on race, religion, ethnic origin, or political opinions. However, he argues, Western states also "cause or contribute the harm that leads to refugee movements". Examples of this are foreign military interventions such as the US and Australian involvement in Indochina in the 1960–1970s, or the Kurdish refugees of the Gulf War. Contributions to refugee movements can also be exacerbated by selling or supplying military arsenal, or political or economic support. Assisting or supporting states which violate the rights of its citizens is not a way to end conflict, but one to aggravate it. Other authors have also referred to neo-liberal economic policies and institutions such as the International Monetary Fund or the World Bank as being another source for the emergence of conflicts, since these are funded by Western countries and established according to its standards (George, 2003). The second assumption refers to the idea that those causing the infliction of harm should be the ones to provide aid, and not the rest. While some may disagree with the later assumption, when the provision of aid does not imply negative consequences or has minor consequences for the state, it seems impossible to define a consistent and convincing argument to fail to provide aid to those individuals fleeing conflict and seeking refuge.

Therefore, the result is one of inflicting pain to vulnerable peoples and failing to defend the liberal values and human rights of the liberal order. It seems as if we are inevitably moving towards the return of a Westphalian system where national security prevails. In the words of Bigo (2008):

> The narrative of "global terrorism" was a way of ending the agonizing effort of trying to make sense of the attacks, of neutralizing the fear of whatever might have been the reason for the attacks. . . . It was a way to discuss the attacks from the standpoint of "answers" instead of questions. Debate was then possible only inside this framework. This framework silenced any discussion about the origins of violence, its political element, its symmetry, and any questioning of the idea that violence is the only way to stop violence.
> (Bigo, 2008)

Conclusion

The securitization of migration is an example of the way states have started addressing international concerns such as migration through the lens of national security and adopting domestic laws and policies. This idea will be presented through the case studies of this book. However, before going into more detail of how states are dealing with migration, it was important to first set the grounds to understand how changes within the international order are also affecting the development of new international norms. As this chapter seeks to demonstrate, states are turning towards national measures to confront international threats. Instead of relying on international norms and multilateral cooperation, there is a preference for advancing national laws and policies to deal with these threats.

Jakob and Luedtke (2018) assert that "the 21st Century nation state is in crisis most directly from external or global forces, and the nature of national responses to these external forces". They further state that while international and supranational institutions have emerged as a result of cooperation between states, these international institutions and international law "now pose a direct challenge to national sovereignty". States have seen certain international cooperation actions turn into foreign interference and control. Globalization has facilitated a freer flow of capital and commodities. It has also become faster and easier for people to travel from one place to another, but migration has become an "obsession" (SIPA, 2022) and managed as a security threat. This "obsession" is reflected in the borders of states. With the fall of the Berlin Wall in 1989, there were only 15 countries with border walls. In 2017, over 70 walls separated nations and states, 50 of which had been constructed after 9/11 (Hayden, 2017; Jones, 2016).

The European Union has been for a long time seen as a human rights promoter. There was a demand and expectation for the EU to address global human rights problems (Balfour, 2008). Yet the EU has also securitized migration more forcefully in the past years. The last step taken has been the agreement of the New Pact on Migration and Asylum in December 2023, a controversial tool that has become "a legitimisation of the EU's anti-immigration policies" (Colomina, 2023), as it has lowered standards and legalized "what hitherto was unequivocally illegal" (Garcés, 2023). The international legal framework was designed to avoid conflict and maintain international security. But the past years have shown that national security is still the core element of liberal states, which shifted their security policies towards protecting the nation instead of the international community. As explained in the previous chapter, there are many events showing the changes within the international order. The securitization of migration is yet another sign that the liberal order is at stake. International norms are in decay, new conflicts are arising, and national security seems to precede human security.

Nonetheless, there are still grounds for hope. As Fukuyama once said, "Historically, we have seen that liberalism is the most attractive when it is threatened" (Illing, 2022). In fact, these same migrants that many dread, are also contributing to resisting autocratic regimes. Escribà-Folch et al. (2022) found that remittances shake two pillars upon which these systems stand. Firstly, remittances from abroad make citizens more independent from their rules. Secondly, diaspora populations have been key to coordinate mobilization and protests in their countries of origin by allowing their citizens, through these remittances, to have the time and means to protest. According to the authors, remittances reshape the balance of power in dictatorships, sometimes even leading to democratic regime change. Therefore, migrants can then be seen as a pivotal part for the promotion of democracy in non-democratic countries, an important value for the spread of liberalism, instead of a threat to the nation. And contrary to some avoid admitting, hostile government policies do not deter migratory flows, but just lead them to take more dangerous journeys.

Therefore, the most valuable way to uphold the liberal system is protecting the rights of the most vulnerable, spreading democratic values and the protection of human rights, including those of migrants. In a world where national security seems to prevail, we cannot look away. The rule of law and the protection of human security should not be ideals, but well-established elements in our system. The following chapters will go deeper into the reasonings behind the securitization of migration. The hope is not to defend the treatment of migration as a security threat, but instead to break down these logics.

References

AJIL. (2018). United States withdraws from the UN Human Rights Council, shortly after receiving criticism about its border policy. *American Journal of International Law*, *112*(4), 745–751.

Avdan, N. (2012). Human trafficking and migration control policy: Vicious or virtuous cycle?, *Journal of Public Policy*, *32*(3), 171–205.

Bacchus, J. (2022, November 9). The Black hole of national security. *CATO Institute*. Retrieved February 6, 2024, from www.cato.org/policy-analysis/black-hole-national-security

Balfour, R. (2008). Human rights promotion. In F. Cerutti & S. Lucarelli (Eds.), *The search for a European identity. Values, policies and legitimacy of the European Union*. Routledge.

Barcos, J. (2024, January 13). La irrelevancia de la UE ante Israel y las contadas voces críticas, demuestran el cambio político en el seno de Europa. *Noticias de Navarra*. Retrieved February 6, 2024, from www.noticiasdenavarra.com/politica/2024/01/13/irrelevancia-ue-israel-contadas-voces-7737976.html

Baylis, E. (2008). National security and political asylum. In A. C. d'Appollonia & S. Reich (Eds.), *Immigration, integration, and security: America and Europe in comparative perspective*. University of Pittsburgh Press.

Bello, V. (2017). *International migration and international security: Why prejudice is a global security threat*. Routledge.

Bigo, D. (2008). The emergence of a consensus: Lobal terrorism, global insecurity, and global security. In A. C. d'Appollonia & S. Reich (Eds.), *Immigration, integration, and security: America and Europe in comparative perspective*. University of Pittsburgh Press.

Bobin, F. (2022, April 1). Cela fait vingt ans que le monde souffre de la dérégulation de la force. *Le Monde*. Retrieved February 6, 2024, from www.lemonde.fr/international/article/2022/04/01/ghassan-salame-cela-fait-vingt-ans-que-le-monde-souffre-de-la-deregulation-de-la-force_6120177_3210.html#xtor=AL-32280270-%5Btwitter%5D-%5Bios%5D

Bogusz, B., Cholewinski, R., Cygan, A., & Szyzczak, E. (2004). *Irregular migration and human rights: Theoretical, European and international perspectives*. Martinus Nijhoff.

Boyle, A., & Chinkin, C. (2007). *The making of international law*. Oxford University Press.

Buhari, M. (2022, September 21). Statement by his excellency Muhammadu Buhari president of the Federal Republic of Nigeria at the general debate of the 77th session of the United Nations general assembly2. *United Nations General Assembly*, 77th Session. Retrieved February 9, 2024, from https://gadebate.un.org/sites/default/files/gastatements/77/ng_en.pdf

Buzan, B., & Hansen, L. (2009). *The evolution of international security studies*. Cambridge University Press.

Buzan, B., Wæver, O., & de Wilde, J. (1998). *Security: A new framework for analysis*. Lyne Rienner Publishers.

Colomina, C. (2023). The world in 2024: Ten issues that will shape the international agenda. *Barcelona Centre for International Affairs (CIDOB)*. Retrieved February 9, 2024, from www.cidob.org/en/publications/publication_series/notes_internacionals/299/the_world_in_2024_ten_issues_that_will_shape_the_international_agenda

Colomina, C., Jar, N., Flores, R., Morales, A., & Morillas, P. (2023, December 13). El mundo en 2024. Los temas que marcarán la agenda internacional. *Live Podcast, CIDOB and Revista 5W*.

Cotachie, S., & Damain, N. (2010). Ratzel and the German geopolitical school: The inception of the culture as an essential element and factor in the political geography. *Revista Română de Geografie Politică*, *12*(2), 298–308.

Creutz, K., Iso-Markku, T., Raik, K., & Tiilikainen, T. (2019). The changing global order and its implications for the EU. *Finnish Institute of International Affairs*, *59*.

Davitti, D. (2019). The rise of private military and security companies in European Union migration policies: Implications under the UNGPs. *Business and Human Rights Journal*, *4*, 33–53.

Duelfer, C. A., & Dyson, S. B. (2011). Chronic misperceptions and international conflict. *International Security*, *36*(1), 73–100.

Dunn, T. J. (2009). *Blockading the border and human rights: The El Paso operation that remade immigration enforcement*. The University of Texas Press.

Eroukhmanoff, C. (2018). Securitissation theory: An introduction. In S. McGlinchey, R. Walters, & C. Scheinpflug (Eds.), *International relations theory*. E-International Relations Publishing.

Escribà-Folch, A., Wright, J., & Covadonga, M. (2022). *Migration and democracy: How remittances undermine dictatorships*. Princeton University Press.

Foot, R. (2005). Human rights and counterterrorism in global governance: Reputation and resistance. *Global Governance*, *11*, 291–310.

Garcés, B. (2023). Migration agreement? *Barcelona Centre for International Affairs (CIDOB)*. Retrieved February 10, 2024, from www.cidob.org/en/publications/publication_series/opinion/2023/migration_agreement

García Segura, C., Pareja, P., & Rodrigo, Á. J. (2019). *La creación de normas globales: entre el cosmopolitismo soft y el resurgir de Westfalia. ORBIS working papers, research group on international law and international relations*. Pompeu Fabra University.

George, S. (2003). Globalizing rights? In M. J. Gibney (Ed.), *Globalizing rights: The Oxford Amnesty lectures 1999*. Oxford University Press.

Gibney, M. J. (2004). *The ethics and politics of asylum. Liberal democracy and the response to refugee*. Cambridge University Press.

Guild, E. (2009). *Security and migration in the 21st century*. Polity Press.

Hayden, S. (2017, January 26). FACTBOX-as Trump moves ahead with the wall, what other countries have border walls? *Thomson Reuters Foundation*. Retrieved February 8, 2024, from https://news.trust.org/item/20170126173018-jq2v7/

Hernández, F. (2022). Geopolítica: Historia, perspectiva y vigencia actual. *Revista de Marina*, *140*(993).

Ibáñez, J. (2016). Actors, authorities, and subjects in a pluralistic global political system. *ORBIS Working Papers*, 2.

IDEA. (2022). The global state of democracy 2022. Forging social contracts in a time of discontent. *International Institute for Democracy and Electoral Assistance*. Retrieved February 8, 2024, from www.idea.int/democracytracker/sites/default/files/2022-11/the-global-state-of-democracy-2022.pdf

IEA. (2023). World energy outlook 2023. *International Energy Agency*. Retrieved February 7, 2024, from www.iea.org/reports/world-energy-outlook-2023?utm_campaign=IEA+newsletters&utm_medium=Email&utm_source=SendGrid

Illing, S. (2022, June 5). The end of history is history. Francis Fukuyama on liberal democracy and its discontents. *Vox*. Retrieved February 10, 2024, from www.vox.com/vox-conversations-podcast/2022/6/6/23060685/vox-conversations-francis-fukuyama-liberalism-and-its-discontents

Jacob, F., & Luedtke, A. (2018). *Migration and the crisis of the modern nation state?* Vernon Press.

Joffé, G. (2008). The European Union, democracy and counter-terrorism in the Maghreb. *Journal of Common Market Studies*, *46*(1), 147–171.

Jones, C., Kilpatrick, J., & Maccanico, Y. (2022). At what cost? Funding the EU's security, defence, and border policies, 2021–2027: A guide for civil society on how EU budget works. *Statewatch and the Transnational Institute*. Retrieved January 10, 2024, from www.statewatch.org/media/3272/at-what-cost-eu-security-budgets-2021-27-sw-tni.pdf

Jones, R. (2016). Borders and walls: Do barriers deter unauthorized migration? *Migration Policy Institute*. Retrieved February 8, 2024, from www.migrationpolicy.org/article/borders-and-walls-do-barriers-deter-unauthorized-migration

Jorgensen, M. (2020). *American foreign policy ideology and the international rule of law. Contesting power through the international criminal court*. Cambridge University Press.

Kaunert, C., & Ezeokafor, E. (2022). *Securitization outside the west. West African security reconceptualised*. Routledge.

Krahmann, E. (2005). *New threats and new actors in international security*. Palgrave Macmillan.

Kreuder-Sonnen, C., & Zangl, B. (2015). Which post-Westphalia? International organizations between constitutionalism and authoritarianism. *European Journal of International Relations*, *21*(3), 568–594.

Krisch, N. (2005). International law in times of hegemony: Unequal power and the shaping of the international legal order. *The European Journal of International Law*, *16*(3), 369–408.

Lacina, B. (2004). From side show to centre stage: Civil conflict after the cold war. *Security Dialogue*, *35*(2).

Mabon, S. (2018). Existential threats and regulating life: Securitization in the contemporary Middle East. *Global Discourse*, *8*(1), 42–58.

Mack, A. (2007). *Global political violence: Explaining the post-cold war decline, coping with crisis working paper series*. International Peace Academy.

Massimino, E. (2017). The border and beyond: The national security implications of migration, refugees, and asylum under U.S. and International Law. In *2017 symposium keynote address protecting refugees: A national security imperative*. Retrieved January 11, 2024, from https://jnslp.com/wp-content/uploads/2018/11/The_Border_and_Beyond_3.pdf

McFate, S. (2015). *The modern mercenary*. Oxford University Press.

Monti, A. (2020, May 7). Coronavirus, come funziona la propaganda cinese. *Formiche.net*. Retrieved January 3, 2024, from https://formiche.net/2020/05/covid-19-cina-usa-video-comunicazione/

Monti, A., & Wacks, R. (2022). *National security in the new world order: Government and the technology of information*. Routledge.

Morgades, S. (2017). Migraciones forzosas y la Unión Europea: la gestión de los flujos como cuestiones de seguridad. In J. Quero, M. Abegón, & S. Morgades (Eds.), *Origen, trayecto y destino la gestión de las migraciones forzosas contemporáneas como desafió a la seguridad en Oriente Medio, en el Mediterráneo y en Europa* (ORBIS Working Paper, Vol. 6). Pompeu Fabra University.

Moser, C. (2022, September 22). The war in Ukraine and its repercussions on Europe's "security and defence constitution". *ConstitutionNet*. Retrieved December 6, 2023, from https://constitutionnet.org/news/war-in-ukraine-repercussions-europe

Pareja-Alcaraz, P. (2010). *Actores y orden en las Relaciones Internacionales. El papel de la República Popular China y Japón en la construcción del orden regional de Asia oriental* [PhD thesis, Pompeu Fabra University, Barcelona].

Peake, J. (2018, April 5–7). *The decline of treaties? Obama, Trump, and the politics of international agreements*. Paper presented at the annual meetings of the Midwest Political Science Association, Chicago.

Planas, L. (2023). Securitizing migration in times of crisis: Private actors and the provision of (in)security. *Cogent Social Sciences*, *10*(1).

Repucci, S., & Slipowitz, A. (2022). The global expansion of authoritarian rule. *Freedom House*. Retrieved February 8, 2024, from https://freedomhouse.org/report/freedom-world/2022/global-expansion-authoritarian-rule

Sending, O. (2022). The war in Ukraine and multilateralism as we know it (Report 7). *Norwegian Institute of International Affairs*.

SIPA. (2022, October 24). Fall 2022 Kent lecture: The deregulation of force with Ghassan Salamé. *Columbia School of International and Public Affairs*.

Slaughter, A.-M. (2007). *The idea that is America: Keeping faith with our calues in a dangerous world*. Basic Books.

Smeltzer, M., & Buyon, N. (2022). From democratic decline to authoritarian aggression. *Freedom House*. Retrieved February 8, 2024, from https://freedomhouse.org/report/nations-transit/2022/from-democratic-decline-to-authoritarian-aggression

The Economist. (2023). *Democracy Index 2022. Frontline democracy and the battle for Ukraine*. The Economist Intelligence Unit Limited.

Ullman, R. (1983). Redefining security. *International Security*, *8*(1), 129–153.

UNDP. (2014). Human development report 1994: Dimensions of human security technical report. *United Nations Development Program*. Retrieved January 11, 2024, from https://hdr.undp.org/content/human-development-report-1994

UNSDG. (2023, December 13). COP28 ends with call to 'transition away' from fossil fuels; UN Chief says phaseout is inevitable. *United Nations Sustainable Development Group*. Retrieved February 7, 2024, from https://unsdg.un.org/latest/stories/cop28-ends-call-'transition-away'-fossil-fuels-un-chief-says-phaseout-inevitable

Vietti, F., & Scribner, T. (2013). Human insecurity: Understanding international migration from a human security perspective. *Journal on Migration and Human Security*, *1*(1), 17–31.

Walia, H. (2021). *Border and rule: Global migration, capitalism and the rise of racist nationalism*. Haymarket Books.

Wessel, R. A. (2011). Informal international law-making as a new form of world legislation? *International Organizations Law Review*, *8*, 253–265.

Whytock, C. A. (2016). *From international law and international relations to law and world politics* (Research Paper no. 2018-29). OC Irvine School of Law.

Wright, T. (2020). One in seven public sector computers still running Windows 7 – CRN FOIs. *CRN Channel Web*. Retrieved January 3, 2024, from www.channelweb.co.uk/news/4009090/seven-public-sector-computers-running-windows-crn-fois

3

Migration

The construction of a security threat

Understanding security studies today

The vision of traditional security studies has become incomplete. The military dimension is still clearly an important one, but it is not the only element in security studies. Traditional security studies adopt an objectivist perspective in the sense that these are about telling what real threats are and how to deal with them. Therefore, this vision was not so much about how to manage security policy and other bureaucratic features, but about military threats and strategies. States are the main unit to consider, and their behavior and interests are seen as objectively 'natural'. It is natural for them to follow the balance of power theory, arms race, or the security dilemma, and thus act accordingly. Later, Critical Security Studies appeared as a critique to this traditional view of security. These studies consider that there can be actors other than the state if they emancipate and have enough power. Rules are not the only structure of the system, but the social world also has an impact on international relations. Environmental or social concerns are also security problems and can thence become security threats. Therefore, this is a wider vision of security studies encompassing various factors beyond the military domain.

There have been different moments in time when specific events have resulted in a revision of security priorities and security threats. The detonation of an atomic bomb on the city of Hiroshima on August 6, 1945, was one of such moments. The Cold War and its ending in 1991 also had important significance in the fields of security and of international relations. And the events of 9/11 became another important historical turning point, and the one this book takes as a landmark. It was then and there that democracy was considered to be at stake. There was a revision of global international security threats, and security was widened to include non-typical security affairs. Security thence changed to a diffusing governmental practice reaching areas such as humanitarian actions, international development, environmental protection, global health, terrorism, or migration, to mention a few.

DOI: 10.4324/9781003458159-4

However, the multiplication of risks also meant that military operations changed in conflict zones. As Huysmans (2014) explains, humanitarian and judicial actions interceded in military operations, changing development action throughout. The European Union and NATO instituted differentiations between divisions, redesigning criminal justice, policing, or counter-insurgency areas, while also repositioning security professionals. These professionals took positions in a wider range of policy areas, linking security more strongly to areas such as international development or migration. This can also be interpreted as another sign that the security domain went beyond the military, and now became a potentially unlimited area where risks could be seen almost everywhere. The limits of security are nowhere to be seen.

This broader understanding of security, as explained in the previous lines, was developed during the 1980s and 1990s. The events of September 11, 2001, were a milestone by which many of these measures were established, and security was formally attached to other areas such as migration. And this widening of securitization became more evident over time, such as with the subsequent bombings in Bali, Madrid, London, and other cities, and the counter-terrorist measures to respond to them. Democracy was said to be threatened by the terrorist threat, and the Global War on Terror was the response to contend it. Per contra, those political and security policies designed to protect democracy and liberal values have seriously undermined civil liberties. To put an example, the privacy of individuals in their own countries has been jeopardized, as the balance between the fundamental right to privacy and national security has tipped in favor of the latter. As Ash put it:

> The hard question now is whether the conduct of the "war against terrorism", in this atmosphere of menace, might not end up being as much a threat to tour own freedoms as terrorism itself.
>
> (Ash, 2002)

On a similar note, Peter Chalk also wrote:

> When dealing with terrorism as a threat to liberal democracy, it is a common assumption that it is the terrorists – who by definition refuse the rules of the liberal democratic "game" – who pose the greatest threat to the underlying principles and freedoms that are enshrined in this form of political life. However, in instances where the state fails to ensure that its response to terrorism is limited, well-defined and controlled, it is likely that institutionalised counter-terrorist policies will pose an even greater threat to the political and civil traditions that are central to the liberal democratic way of life.
>
> (Chalk, 1998)

The difference is that Ash's article was written in the aftermath of 9/11, while Chalk's publication was written in 1998, three years before the terrorist attacks. Chalk's warning was based on national cases, studying the measures that the Italian government took against the 'Brigata Rossa' (Red Brigades) in the 1970s, or those of Spain to respond to the terrorist action of Euskadi Ta Askatasuna (ETA). Nevertheless, the idea that the government's response to terrorism needs to be applied considering the involvement of the rights of individuals is maintained. And doubts or concerns on whether they are protected or not still remain.

Instead, what we have seen is that securitization practices have strengthened in the past years, being almost expected, and naturalized. In this sense, a challenge arises from the fact that the more issues are securitized, the more there is an expectation that exceptional measures be adopted to contend (Lucarelli et al., 2020). And politics have contributed to this vision, presenting the world as insecure. Security is not just a set of policies or actions designed to *contend* a threat. Security has become so politicized that the mere mentioning of the word *creates* the threat. Security practices have thus become political practices. While the role of mitigating threats to protect the political community is the role of those in power, politicians and the political elite are not just the ones establishing the mechanisms but are also the ones determining what is a security threat to the state or to society.

As explained by Huysmans (2014):

> Democracy is a political stake in security practice, not simply because of fundamental rights being violated in the name of security but because security practice inherently organises social and political relations around enemies, risks, fear, anxiety. When insecurities pervade how we relate to our neighbours, how we perceive international politics, how governments formulate policies, at stake is not our security but our democracy.
>
> (Huysmans, 2014)

The migration crisis of 2015

Bello (2017b) grasps the brutality of the so-called migration crisis of 2015 through an image that today remains in the memory of many:

> The sad photo of a small Syrian child washed ashore in Greece on 2 September 2015 suddenly came to symbolize for European societies the cruelty that both conflicts and the European hardening of borders represent for the most vulnerable.
>
> (Bello, 2017b)

That image did not only show the enduring conditions of their trips. It also manifested the cruelty of European societies, increasing border control precisely to prevent these peoples from seeking refuge in European territory.

The situation worsened that Summer of 2015, when migratory flows increased. European states, vanquished by the great number of refugees arriving to southern states and making their way up to northern Europe, started looking for measures to stop these flows of peoples. Borders were strengthened, and states started looking for ways to control incoming migration flows, patrolling the seas and returning boats to the countries where they had departed from. At the same time, new transit routes appeared, and now migrants were also going through Hungary to reach European land. Overwhelming migratory flows used the deficiencies in Hungarian reception capacities to then arrive at other Member States like Austria or Germany. The Eastern Mediterranean Route became a favored entry point, and an important number of irregular entries into the European Union were arriving through the western Balkans. The flows of migrants were so big that European Union Member States reacted by increasing border control in an effort to keep them out. And Europe, which was just in the aftermath of a global financial crisis, was now dealing with unprecedented numbers of incoming asylum seekers and refugees. The arrival of these migrants along with the strict policies which had resulted in restricting economic and social policies, led to an upsurge of far-right ideologies and xenophobia. The European Union, erected as the symbol of liberalism, was now closing borders and limiting the rights of vulnerable groups.

Right before Summer, in May 2015, the EU issued an 'Implementation Package', part of the Agenda on Migration, to relieve migratory pressures on frontline states by establishing a relocation plan among all Member States. This temporary relocation scheme was proposed on the basis of Article 78(3) of the Treaty on the Functioning of the European Union (TFEU). This First Implementation Package planned to triple the capacities of the European Agency for the Management of Operational Cooperation at the External Borders of the Member States of the European Union's (Frontex) joint operations Triton and Poseidon. Deployments were increased to support Italian authorities controlling the sea. But because of the higher incoming numbers of migrants through these routes during the Summer period, a Second Implementation Package was issued in September 2015.

The perceived security situation was aggravated by the policy rhetoric emphasizing the 'external' challenge posed by these migrant influxes. An image of Greece as being incapable of controlling its borders was spread, which led to the introduction of temporary internal border controls in the EU. The aims of the Second Implementation Package were not so much on the protection of those travelling by sea, but the narrative changed towards one directed to controlling movement within the Schengen area (Ceccorulli, 2012).

The Third Implementation Package did not take long to arrive and was put forward in December of that same year. Again, emphasis was placed on the protection of Schengen through external border management. A European Border and Coast Guard were created, while the hotspot system and the relocation scheme were accelerated to alleviate the burden on southern states. Collective securitization was already taking place. And even in this multilateral approach to increase control at EU's external borders, many Member States like Austria, Hungary, Germany, Slovenia, and Sweden decided to reintroduce or maintain temporary controls through their internal borders. States were using national border control to contend an external threat, regardless of the measures already taking place at the EU level. This national response was seen as fundamental, showing a conscious choice to make national interests prevail.

The term 'European refugee crisis' started being widely used in April 2015, when five boats sank in the Mediterranean Sea while trying to reach European shores. There was an estimated death toll of 1,222 people out of 2,000 of those who were in the boats (Baerwaldt, 2018). Almost 5.2 million refugees and migrants reached Europe by the end of 2016 (UNHCR, 2017). These great numbers of peoples flooded the capacity of the asylum systems of southern European states, and the Union in general. Transit countries such as Turkey and Libya and their national emergency responses capacities have been overwhelmed by the number of incoming refugees. This 'refugee crisis' has also been called many times the 'European refugee crisis', when 40% of the 60 million displaced people worldwide come from the Arab region, and mainly Syria (UNHCR, 2018). Many of Syrian refugees have fled to Lebanon and Jordan, also overflowing their national systems, and taking even larger numbers of refugees than Europe. But it was only when the capacity to deal with refugees and asylum seekers at the EU's southern border countries such as Greece, Italy, and Spain collapsed, that the idea of a 'refugee crisis' emerged.

However, while the European Union was talking about a 'refugee crisis', Chetail (2016) points out that even though asylum applications had widely increased a few years before, the 1.2 million applications of asylum seekers in 2015 represented only 0.2% of the whole EU population. And if we bring these figures to the broader picture, and compare them with other regions of the world, it is even more evident that the EU is not the region to deal with most refugee flows. Data show that in 2015, the Global South hosted 86% of the world's refugees (Chetail, 2016), a tendency which has been maintained as in 2022, 85% of the world's displaced people were still moving to other developing countries (UNHCR, 2021).

This leaves one to wonder whether this so-called refugee crisis is about the refugee flows themselves or about the European Union migration system and its willingness to deal with such an important number of incoming migrants. From the one hand, receiving systems in southern European states failed, and on the other, northern European states have failed to support them. The absence of rule of law in the admission of migrants and of integration policies has undermined public confidence in their authority's management criteria, and this in turn has fueled populist movements with radical ideas. They untruthfully talk about the socioeconomic impact that immigration causes in their countries, and in some cases fake news is spread to support anti-immigrant discourses. Calling a 'disturbance' a 'crisis' can be a means to justify radical action, and this is what populist parties do to justify their actions (UH, 2018).

As put by Walia (2021):

> Language such as "migrant crisis", and the often-corresponding "migrant invasion", is a pretext to shore up further border securitization and repressive practices of detention and deportation. Such representations depict migrants and refugees as the *cause* of an *imagined* crisis at the border, when, in fact, mass migration is the outcome of the actual crises of capitalism, conquest, and climate change.
>
> (Walia, 2021)

Migration as a security threat

Migration has been presented as a security threat from a wide range of sectors. It is now time to try to detail the reasoning behind this logic and the different arguments used by securitizing actors to justify the establishment of a link between migration and security.

To further explain this connection to security among different sectors of life, the 'migration threat' is studied from six different areas, studying migration as a threat: (1) to national identity, (2) to the economy, (3) to the welfare state, (4) to bilateral relations, (5) to the public order, and (6) to national security. It must be noted that the line between some of these factors may blur and that some areas may overlap, presenting migration as a security threat to both, for instance, the economy and the welfare state. Nonetheless, in this section these will be presented separately to provide a more specific understanding of the grounds behind securitization discourses. Offering a global overview of migration as a threat from different perspectives will also help determine whether in some cases these arguments are objectively justified or whether migration is presented as a threat following different advantages.

Firstly, securitization can be a response to contend the threat that migrants pose to the national identity of a collective. As explained by Huntington (1996), migration can be seen as a danger to national tradition and societal homogeneity, acting as a trigger of social and political disintegration. Following this view, multiculturalism is seen as a barrier to maintain local cultural identity. The War on Terror and the terrorist attacks that followed on Western soil have fostered nationalist discourses which point to migration as the source of fragmentation of societies, precisely because the perpetrators of 9/11 were not nationals and matched a certain profile. The terrorist was portrayed as one with a concrete ethnicity, and securitizing discourses were quickly directed against immigration and being pointed to as the biggest threat to national identity.

In Switzerland, for instance, political discourses against migration and towards the protection of Swiss national identity have raised progressively throughout the last years by using the *Überfremdung*'s concept in public debates to refer to "a foreign overpopulation threatening the Swiss identity" (Riaño & Wastl-Walter, 2006). In the United Kingdom, there was a campaign in 2013 to encourage irregular immigrants to leave the country voluntarily. Vans carrying posters with the message "In the UK illegally? Go home or face arrest" circulated around London for weeks. In 2023, a new advertising campaigned was also launched, this time with the intention to deter Albanian nationals from making the journey to the UK. For this occasion, the line was "Enter the UK illegally and you could be relocated to a safe third country", referring to the government's plan to send asylum seekers to Rwanda (Reid, 2023).

For many, religious beliefs and practices are a fundamental part of their life, being the main element defining their cultural identity and being inseparable from social existence. The cultural clash between nationals and those coming from abroad may not be troublesome in some countries, but it can be a risk in those where there already are ethnic, religious, or cultural conflicts. Therefore, in countries where there is already a certain degree of social detachment, the arrival of migrants may be seen as a greater risk to national identity. Nationals may see their languages, values, norms, and customs challenged with the arrival of immigration. And instead of seeing multiculturalism as a way to enrich a country, it is rather seen as a threat.

Secondly, migration can be seen as a threat to the economy. Immigrant movements have also increased as migrants are looking for better economic opportunities far from their countries of origin. This has been used by many politicians to advance anti-immigration discourses arguing that immigration is a problem to the economic stability of the country and accusing them of being the source of unemployment among nationals. The statement on immigrants "stealing jobs" has been heard rather frequently in many countries.

During Trump's presidential campaign, and before he was first elected, his discourses often contributed to this view. In Phoenix, he accused immigrants of "Taking our jobs. They're taking our manufacturing jobs. They're taking our money. They're killing us" (Schreckinger, 2015). In another speech given in Las Vegas in 2019, he said, "Working-class Americans are left to pay the price for mass illegal immigration: reduced jobs, lower wages, overburdened schools, hospitals that are so crowded you can't get in, increased crime, and a depleted social safety net" (Lach, 2019). Nevertheless, as many have continuously affirmed, this is far from the truth, as most undocumented migrants often do the jobs that many natives are not willing to do. Shortly after Trump's 2019 discourse, three Harvard University economists released a paper exploring the impact of immigration in multiple countries including the United States. They argued that restricting immigration, as Donald Trump wanted to do, would probably weaken economic growth, as migration was needed to sustain the level of the population given the low birth rates in the country. They also realized that while native-born Americans thought that immigrants made up to 36% of the total US population, the net flow of migration was actually about 0.3%, immigrants making a total of 13% of the population. The real figure was therefore almost three times less than what Americans would have guessed (Boak, 2019).

The truth is that most undocumented workers often do the jobs many natives are not willing to do. And as many economists have argued, immigrants are not an economic threat to the host country but they actively contribute to sustaining the economy (Enchautegui, 2015; Hoban, 2017; World Bank, 2018; IMF, 2020). However, in periods of recession, an antipathetic view of immigration is widely spread throughout, leading to a disapproval and negative consciousness towards migrant communities. The perception of immigrants as an economic burden can then unchain a bad perception of immigration as an economic threat. This, in turn, complicates their integration into the new society, as they are seen as unwanted competitors taking the job opportunities of the nationals and taking an unfair advantage of public goods.

Moreover, migrants can also be perceived as a threat to the economy depending on the existing political regime. Globalization involves the movement of goods, services, and capital, but also of people across borders. There are different motivations determining if and where a migrant will go. One element to take into consideration when talking about these movements, is the type of political regime of the country. Most may think that democracies receive more migrants and that these are coming from non-democratic countries. However, a study by Breunig et al. (2012) shows that democratic regimes accommodate fewer immigrants than autocracies and that more people emigrate from democracies than from autocracies. What is more, it is in most liberal democracies where there is a higher anti-immigration feeling, probably because other types of regimes are able to grant fewer rights to foreign workers since they are less concerned with civil rights, but also because they have more flexible labor markets. That is why many economic migrants looking for jobs will go to other state-systems, since these offer more guest worker programs and because those ruling the country are less constrained by popular xenophobic demand. On the other side, these types of regimes are less likely to allow their citizens to leave the country but instead try to retain them. As the authors of this study, say

> at the individual level, the search for economic well-being trumps any aspiration for the political freedoms offered by democracy. At the macro-level, it is important to recognize that democracies tend to block entry and allow exits, while non-democracies tend to block exits and allow entry.

Thirdly, and connecting to the previous point, migration is also perceived as a threat to the welfare state. In periods of economic recessions and of higher unemployment rates when there is more scarcity, immigrants are discerned as the competitors of nationals in the fight for social goods. Some locals see them as illegitimate actors having no right to access national social assistance and are unwilling to offer them protection. Immigrants are accused of taking advantage of public resources and thus being a threat to the welfare system and for those nationals who want to access it. Another common claim is that the social expenditure of migrants is higher than the economic contribution that they make to the system. They are thence blamed for the implementation of welfare restrictions or the erosion of the system as a whole, even though welfare instability is not a result of migration.

The Spanish case can be an example of the unbalance between the perception of the population and the economic contribution of migrant groups. Studies have shown that even after the 2008 financial crisis, the population of immigrant origin did not make an intensive use of social protection systems. Even then, the fiscal balance between their contribution to the economy and the cost of the social services they used was clearly favorable to the state (Moreno & Bruquetas, 2011). Later, the situation has been similar, studies showing that their access to welfare benefits was equal or even inferior to those of the national population, and thence not proving this overuse of social services that some securitization discourses have used (Muñoz de Bustillo & Grande, 2017). In contrast, some still believe that migration is one of the most important sources for national economic burdens. Extreme right-wing political party Vox, in its electoral program for the 2023 national elections, put migration as one of the central policies of its political program. They put forward the idea to make sure that no irregular migrant could receive any kind of social service while harshening procedures and requirements to regularize their status, precisely to make sure that they do not benefit from public resources (Vox, 2023). Similar is the situation of Italy, where Georgia Meloni, candidate of far-right Brothers of Italy, won the 2022 elections with similar ideas.

Fourthly, migrants can also be perceived as a threat to the host country in regard to the bilateral relations established with the country of origin. Weiner (1992) explains that there are different reasons why bilateral relations can be endangered when there are refugees in-between. He argues that when refugees are opposed to the regime of their country and it is recognized that there is a well-founded fear of persecution, the host country is somehow accusing the country of origin to engage in persecution, and so it is saying that there is a justification to be morally opposing to the regime. Thus, just by granting asylum a state may create a more hostile relationship with another nation. An example of this can be found in the US Congress debate in January 1990 on whether Chinese students should be permitted to remain in the US because of the possible persecutions that could face in China. Hosting this debate was seen by the People's Republic of China as an interference in its internal affairs. When host countries actively support refugees in their fight with the country of origin, they become a tool of inter-state conflict. Hence the way in which governments assess and respond to refugee claims can, for instance, potentially lead to a clash between the two.

Irregular migration flows and large refugee movements can also lead to other tensions between origin countries and destination and/or transit countries. The latter may use irregular migration as a negotiation card to force destination countries to make political, commercial, and other economic concessions, while destination countries want to expulse unwanted immigration back to where they came from. Tensions of this kind have arisen in different regions: between the Albanian Government and the European Union, or between the United States and Mexico.

Fifthly, migration is presented as a threat to public order. In this sense, the link that some political groups and media outlets establish between crime and migration hinders the integration of migrants within the host country. The perception that migrants are more frequently involved in drug trafficking, thefts and robberies, armed aggressions, or terrorism has been strengthened not only since 9/11 but also in the aftermath of every other terrorist attack since 2001. The involvement of some immigrants in criminal activities has led to using prejudicial stereotyping in public debates connecting immigration with criminal threats. Adjudicating security connotations related to terrorism and international crime to the area of migration is now more common than ever, regardless of whether the perpetrators of the attacks were citizens born in that same country.

The language used to refer to incoming migrants as "illegal migrants", contributes to creating a negative perception of migration. And those in detention centers for their undocumented condition and illegal entry into the country are considered criminals. The citizenry will never know the reason why each of these migrants has been detained, whether there has been a serious offence, or whether this has been due to lack of valid documentation. Furthermore, while long-term migration increases positive attitudes towards migration, short-term migration increases prejudice as it reinforces the view that migrants arrive and leave the country continuously (Bello, 2017a). Therefore, these types of administrative routines deriving from a securitization process often translate into more negative views towards newcomers (Bello, 2017b).

In practice, this means that decision-making in the area of migration is moving away from the human rights perspective to a vision involving the protection of the country. It is in this way that migration is moved from the humanitarian field to one involving national security. And words like 'migrant', 'foreigner', and 'refugee' are now more frequently connected to security and are powerful signifiers in contemporary Europe (Huysmans,

2000; Greimas & Courtés, 1993). Migration has simply become a security matter, frequently connected to crime and public order issues.

Finally, migration can also be perceived as a national security threat, mostly referring to the terrorist phenomenon. Since 9/11, the Bali bombings, and the Mombasa and Kenya attacks, national security has strongly been linked to matters of border control. Especially relevant is the first of these events, as it created a precedent which transformed the association of the foreigner with the terrorist threat. Migration and border control have since then been used as justified means to prevent more terrorist attacks.

Even though the West has faced a clear intensification of terrorist attacks after 9/11, liberal democracies are less prone to terrorist attacks than other regime types. A study by Magen (2018) reports that the higher the quality of the democracy and the more civil liberties are guaranteed, the less likely it is for that country to suffer terrorist incidents. In 2013, countries like Bahrain, Iran, Kuwait, Somalia, South Sudan, and Sudan had multiplied by more than 7,000% the likelihood of suffering terrorist attacks than in 2002. The presence of groups like the Islamic State in Iraq and Syria, Boko Haram, or Al-Qaeda affiliates are more often seen in fragile states, where they have conducted most of their operations. And it is precisely in these contexts of state fragility where they find more ways to spread extremist ideas. Corruption, repression, poor governance, inadequate public services, and lack of accountability are all factors contributing to the rise of extremism and facilitating the recruitment of new members to terrorist groups. State security capacity is not strong enough in these societies. And wherever there are security vacuums, they can more easily exert their control over local populations (Yacoubian & Stares, 2005; EER, 2023). Still, Western countries are the ones who have quickly reacted to the terrorist threat by adapting national security agendas based on the securitization of migration and Islam, resulting in the damage of the normal functioning of democracy and multicultural values.

Migration can thence be presented as a security threat according to at least these six potential 'justifications'. The elite in power, with the help of the media, are the ones often presenting immigrants as a security threat following one or more of these views. One or another may prevail according to the previous existing values of the society, the historical context and recent events or problems in the country. Hence migration can be seen as a threat to the economy or the welfare state in a country, but as a threat to national identity in another. There is usually a combination of different threats, as migrants can be presented as a threat to multiple aspects of one country, although often times there will be one sticking out among the others, given the social, political, and economic context of the country at a given time. Migration according to these six potential threats can be summarized in the following table:

Table 3.1 Migration-threat justifications

Potential threat	*Justification/Rationalization*	*Example*
To national identity	Clash between multiculturalism and nationalism. Nationals may see their languages, values, norms, and customs challenged with the arrival of immigration. The priority is the preservation of the national cultural identity.	The case of Switzerland where political discourses have raised the need to protect national identity towards immigration ("*Überfremdung*'s).
To the economy	Migration as an economic burden, associated with the scarcity of social and economic benefits for its nationals. Dependent on the political regime.	The repeated message that immigrants are stealing the jobs of nationals. This idea has been repeated throughout, including Trump's presidential campaign.
To the welfare state	Immigrants as illegitimate actors using social goods and accessing national social assistance. Intensified feeling/threat when the country is in economic recession.	Political ideas considering the migrant community as a burden to the national housing market as seen in New Zealand.
To bilateral relations	Especially when there are refugees involved. If supporting these refugees, the host country can be seen as accusing the country of origin of engaging in persecution and, in some cases, opposing its political regime.	The debate in the United States on whether to allow Chinese students to stay in the country. This was perceived as a hostile move by the People's Republic of China.
To the public order	Connecting crime and migration. Frequently seen in areas like drug trafficking, thefts and robberies, armed aggressions, and terrorism.	Public messages from politicians and the media connecting migrant groups to crime and security issues. This is now commonly seen in many Western countries.
To national security	Association of the foreigner with terrorism. New political and media discourses have led to a new security agenda based on the securitization of Islam, especially seen in the West.	Many of today's security agendas are based on the securitization of Islam. This has been the case of the United States and European countries.

Whichever justifications are used to securitize migration in a given context, the linkage between migration and security has aggravated the general public perception of the migrant community. Immigration attitudes vary across countries, but it seems fair to assert that the perception of immigration by the West has been generally negative for many years now, which has contributed to advancing a general practice to securitize migration.

Migration and terrorism in the 21st century

As long as something poses a vital threat to society, whether this threat pertains to the military domain or not, the issue can become securitized. Furthermore, as previously explained, today security studies have a larger framework that has expanded the security agenda to include other sectors than the traditional military ones, although national security remains an important one.

One of the national and international security threats which have most often been connected to migration in recent decades is that in relation to international terrorism. And in the aftermath of the events of 9/11, this connection became particularly strong, as political leaders started talking about the start of a global war. It was thus after the attacks of 2001 on US soil, when President George W. Bush was the one to declare that the attack was an act of "war", and so a "War on Terror" against terrorism was the only possible response, calling for other nations to be "either for us or against us" (The Guardian, 2001). No one wanted to be seen as the enemy of the United States, and so countries joined efforts to counter the terrorist threat. Even NATO invoked the mutual defense clause for the first time in its history (NATO, 2001). Years later, and after every terrorist attack in a Western country, there is still talk about the international war on terrorism and the need to protect countries from potential terrorists threatening security.

Modern terrorism in Europe can be traced back to the 1970s, when there were different terrorist groups in different European countries (Bossong, 2013). In Spain there was the Euskadi Ta Askatasuna (ETA), a separatist terrorist group, while in the United Kingdom the Irish Republican Army (IRA) was created with a similar intent. The Red Brigades in Italy and the Red Army Faction in West Germany were left-wing terrorist organizations. While within the period between the 1970s and the 1990s there were not the same number of casualties as with the New York City attacks of 2001 or with the Madrid bombings of 2004, this was also a period of mass killings (Kaunert & Léonard, 2019). Yet the latest wave of securitization measures – which has been extended to this day – did not emerge until the September 11 attacks. That was the incident that led to the securitization of migration of the 21st century.

Before then, there were various terrorist groups in different states, but they were dealt with at the national level only. It was not until 9/11 that international counter-terrorist cooperation arose. The events of that day were of such a scale and impact that a new international threat emerged from then one. Four planes were hijacked by Al-Qaeda terrorist members. Two of these planes were flown into the Twin Towers in New York City, a third plane hit the Pentagon, and the fourth crashed in Pennsylvania. The images of the World Trade Center were broadcasted in mass media and played around the world. The character of the terrorist threat changed that day. Kaunert and Léonard explain the importance of these events for collective securitization:

> In this sense, 9/11 was a single precipitating event for the collective securitisation of terrorism in the EU. The terrorist attacks on that occasion were uniquely grave in character and while they occurred far from Europe, they reinforced the growing perception that Western governments now faced a new terrorist threat, which was far more concerning than the threat that had been posed by left-wing or ethno-nationalist terrorist groups. This is not to say that the numerous Islamist terrorist attacks that happened later in Europe, including in Madrid, London, Paris, Brussels and Nice, did not have any impact on the EU counter-terrorism policy, for they certainly did. However, from an analytical viewpoint, these can be seen as belonging to the final stage of the collective securitisation framework.
>
> (Kaunert & Léonard, 2019)

The association of terrorism with war shows the gravity of the perception of terrorism as a serious security threat, and this in turn ended up justifying the application of emergency measures. As explained by Tsoukala (2008):

> Since wartime is traditionally associated with sacrifices and pain, people are expected to accept emergency rules as a necessary sacrifice to be made on the altar of their effective protection. . . . At the same time, the comparison of terrorism with war produces a normalization effect insofar as it draws parallels to previous wars and, consequently, includes the present threat in a familiar context of past exceptional situations.
>
> (Tsoukala, 2008)

In a paper by Hülsse and Spencer (2008), the authors argued that the focus of terrorist studies should not only be placed in the terrorist as an actor, but in the terrorist discourse. They studied media discourses in Germany in the context of Al-Qaeda, realizing that they went from presenting the terrorist group from a military to a criminal organization. Their analysis concludes that if there are no terrorist attacks in the country for an extended period of time it is harder to connect an existence of a threat within society. At the same time, Germany's previous experience with a war is a very different one from the one characterized by the War on Terror. Again, this makes discourses on the war against terrorism harder to represent in the German population. Instead, since crime is a common phenomenon in all societies, terrorism started being presented in the context of a criminal organization instead of a military threat. By changing the metaphor, that is, by changing the discourse, the experience and perception of the population towards terrorism were also changed. At the same time, this discourse shift transformed Al-Qaeda from an external to an internal threat. And again, the securitization of migration is brought to the table. In sum, when states want to connect migration to security, they find a way to do so. And with different justifications, migration is easily and rapidly presented as a security threat among the population.

Conclusion

In the 21st century, migration has arisen as one of the most prominent security threats, as expressed by politicians and the media, and this is mainly given due to the terrorist threat. In the aftermath of the terrorist attacks of 9/11 in the United States, terrorism became one of the most important security threats, not only for the national security of the US, but also for international security. As the Security Council stated in Resolution 1566, "terrorism in all its forms and manifestations constitutes one of the most serious threats to peace and security".[1]

During the 2007–2008 financial crisis, there was another upturn in anti-immigrant sentiment in many countries, as migrants were then blamed for economic regression, lack of jobs, and economic cutbacks across Europe. And during the Covid-19 pandemic they were again blamed for spreading the disease (Planas, 2024). However, many seem to forget that the reality is that many of these migrants are not even going to Western countries, but they are fleeing elsewhere. And if they are leaving their homes it is out of need, not because of want. Conflicts in countries like Libya, Syria, and Yemen have brought devastation and great suffering to their populations, and as a response, many have decided to flee their countries searching for safety elsewhere. As a result, refugee waves have increased in the past years, some of which have arrived in Europe. Instead of trying to protect these peoples in their dangerous journeys or protecting them at home, the response of the West has been to point at these refugees coming from Africa and the Middle East as security threats to their own states. Again, we seem to be moving further away from liberal values and from providing human security. Instead, national security has again taken the stage in a world dominated by national interests and other geopolitical and economic concerns.

References

Ash, T. G. (2002, October 17). In the terror trap. *The Guardian*. Retrieved July 22, 2023, from www.theguardian.com/world/2002/oct/17/september11.uk

1 Security Council Resolution 1566 (2004, October 8). *Concerning threats to international peace and security caused by terrorism*, S/RES/1566 (2004).

Baerwaldt, N. (2018). *The European refugee crisis: Crisis for whom?* Faculty of Law Blogs: Border Criminologies, University of Oxford.
Bello, B. (2017a). Migraciones, Seguridad Nacional y Seguridad Humana: un nuevo modelo migratorio para luchar contra el prejuicio como reto a la seguridad global. In *Monografías 152. Las migraciones internacionales, percepción y realidad. Un análisis desde la perspectiva de la seguridad*. Escuela Superior de las Fuerzas Armadas.
Bello, V. (2017b). *International migration and international security: Why prejudice is a global security threat*. Routledge.
Boak, J. (2019, February 8). AP fact check: Trump plays on immigration myths. *PBS NewsHour*. Retrieved July 20, 2023, from www.pbs.org/newshour/politics/ap-fact-check-trump-plays-on-immigration-myths
Bossong, R. (2013). *The evolution of EU counter-terrorism: European security policy after 9/11*. Routledge.
Breunig, C., Cao, X., & Luedtke, A. (2012). Global migration and political regime type: A democratic disadvantage. *British Journal of Political Science*, *42*(4), 825–854.
Ceccorulli, M. (2012). Back to Schengen: The collective securitization of the EU free-border area. In S. Lucarelli, L. Van Langenhove, & J. Wouters (Eds.), *The EU and multilateral security governance*. Routledge.
Chalk, P. (1998). The response to terrorism as a threat to liberal democracy. *Australian Journal of Politic and History*, *44*(3), 373–388.
Chetail, V. (2016). Migration and international law: A short introduction. In V. Chetail (Ed.), *International law and migration* (Vol. 1). Edward Elgar Publishing.
EER. (2023). Mona Yacoubian: Ideology is just one of the many drivers of terrorism. *European Eye on Radicalization*. Retrieved July 21, 2023, from https://eeradicalization.com/mona-yacoubian-ideology-is-just-one-of-the-many-drivers-of-terrorism/
Enchautegui, M. E. (2015). *Immigrant and native workers compete for different low-skilled jobs*. Urban Institute.
Greimas, A. J., & Courtés, J. (1993). *Sémiotique. Dictionnaire raisonné de la théorie du langage*. Hachette.
Hoban, B. (2017). Do immigrants "steal" jobs from American workers? *The Brookings Institution*. Retrieved July 20, 2023, from www.brookings.edu/articles/do-immigrants-steal-jobs-from-american-workers/
Hülsse, R., & Spencer, A. (2008). The metaphor of terror: Terrorism studies and the constructivist turn. *Security Dialogue*, *39*(6), 571–592.
Huntington, S. P. (1996). *The clash of civilizations*. Simon & Schuster.
Huysmans, J. (2000). The European Union and the securitization of migration. *Journal of Common Market Studies*, *38*(5).
Huysmans, J. (2014). *Security unbound. Enacting democratic limits*. Routledge.
International Monetary Fund (IMF). (2020, April). *Word economic outlook*. Author.
Kaunert, C., & Léonard, S. (2019). The collective securitisation of terrorism in the European Union. *West European Politics*, *42*(2), 261–277.
Lach, E. (2019). Trump's dangerous scapegoating of immigrants at the state of union. *The New Yorker*. Retrieved July 20, 2023, from www.newyorker.com/news/current/trumps-dangerous-scapegoating-of-immigrants-at-the-state-of-the-union
Lucarelli, S., Sperling, J., & Webber, M. (2020). *Collective securitisation and security governance in the European Union*. Routledge.

Magen, A. (2018). Fighting terrorism: The democracy advantage. *Journal of Democracy*, *29*(1), 111–125.

Moreno, F. J., & Bruquetas, M. (2011). *Inmigración y Estado del bienestar en España. Colección Estudios Sociales*. Num. 31. Obra Social "la Caixa".

Muñoz de Bustillo, R., & Grande, R. (2017). *Inmigración y Estado de Bienestar en España*. CIDOB.

NATO. (2001, December 5). *Countering terrorism*. North Atlantic Treaty Organization. Retrieved July 17, 2023, from https://www.nato.int/cps/en/natohq/topics_77646.htm

Planas, L. (2024). Securitizing migration in times of crisis: Private actors and the provision of (in)security. *Cogent Social Sciences*, *10*(1).

Reid, S. (2023, May 5). UK government launches ad campaign to deter Albanian migrants. *Euronews*. Retrieved July 17, 2023, from www.euronews.com/2023/05/30/uk-government-launches-advertising-campaign-to-put-off-migrants-from-albania

Riaño, Y., & Wastl-Walter, D. (2006). Immigration policies and discourses on foreigners and the politics of identity in Switzerland. *Environment and Planning A*, *38*(9), 1693–1713.

Schreckinger, B. (2015, July 11). Donald Trump storms phoenix. *Politico*. Retrieved July 20, 2023, from www.politico.com/story/2015/07/donald-trump-storms-phoenix-119989

The Guardian. (2001, September 14). *Bush's new world order*. Retrieved July 18, 2023, from https://www.theguardian.com/world/2001/sep/14/september11.usa6

Tsoukala, A. (2008). Defining the terrorist threat in the post-September 11 era. In D. Bigo & A. Tsoukala (Eds.), *Terror, insecurity, and liberty* (pp. 49–99). Routledge.

University of Helsinki (UH). (2018). *A crisis begins when we call it a crisis. News and Press Releases*. Author.

UNHCR. (2017). Refugee crisis in Europe. *United Nations High Commissioner for Refugees*. Retrieved January 14, 2024, from www.unrefugees.org/emergencies/refugee-crisis-in-europe/

UNHCR. (2018). Global trends: Forced displacement in 2018. *United Nations High Commissioner for Refugees*. Retrieved January 14, 2024, from www.unhcr.org/figures-at-a-glance.html

UNHCR. (2021). UNHCR global trends 2021. *United Nations High Commissioner for Refugees*. Retrieved January 14, 2024, from www.unhcr.org/flagship-reports/globaltrends/globaltrends2019/

Vox. (2023). Programa electoral para las elecciones generales. *Vox*. Retrieved July 20, 2023, from www.voxespana.es/programa/programa-electoral-vox

Walia, H. (2021). *Border and rule: Global migration, capitalism and the rise of racist nationalism*. Haymarket Books.

Weiner, M. (1992). Security, stability, and international migration. *International Security*, *17*(3), 91–126.

World Bank. (2018). *Mixed migration, forced displacement and job outcomes in South Africa*. Author.

Yacoubian, M., & Stares, P. (2005). *Rethinking the war on terror*. U.S. Institute of Peace.

The securitization of migration and the prevalence of national security

Theoretical framework

As security studies evolved from the traditional realist vision, critics argued that non-military elements could also be of great importance to security studies. Many academics supporting this idea started a subfield called Critical Security Studies, a term that was coined during a conference at York University in 1994 and became the title of a book produced after the event. There is no single theory within this subfield, but constructivism became an important theoretical framework, and it has also been a foundation for the theory of securitization, as they both focus on social processes. Constructivism is concerned with the ways in which identities are formed, as these attach meanings to different material objects. The importance is thus placed on the human interpretation of events. Securitization studies, on the other hand, focuses on the process under which an element can become a security concern. And the Copenhagen School, one of the strands of Critical Security Studies, was the one to develop the notion of 'securitization'. Buzan et al. (1998) were the ones to develop securitization theory in their book *People, States and Fear*, acknowledging the importance of human and social processes on the construction of security threats.

Migration and borders became an important area for constructionist understandings of security. In the 1990s, refugee policy and mass migration grew into key human security concerns (Huysmans & Squire, 2017). But in the field of international relations, scholars have different views on what they believe has driven the securitization of migration. Following a realist anarchical position, some have argued that Western states should fear the "coming anarchy" associated with big migration flows (Huntington, 2004). Neoliberalists contend that structural threat environment is the primary factor explaining securitization (Rudolph, 2003). Others believe that the securitization process is the result of routinized practices by the professionals of security (Bigo, 2002, 2008).

The present book agrees with this wider notion and study of security, as values and beliefs are structural characteristics of societies and therefore have a meaningful impact on both social and political action. The material world is

DOI: 10.4324/9781003458159-5

defined and interpreted by humans, and so is security. Identities can shape state action, and norms are also influenced by interests, values, and even identities of actors. Therefore, it is through the interpretation of events that individuals construct their own perception and understanding of what a security threat is. Consequently, the thoughts in this book depart from a constructivist perspective of security, and it recognizes the important work of Barry Buzan, Ole Wæver, and Jaap de Wilde, especially following their work on developing the notion of 'securitization'. Securitization is a result of human interpretation. As these authors argue, "security is a quality actors inject into issues by securitizing them" (Buzan et al., 1998). Ole Wæver was the one to center the focus on the speech act, a key element for securitization theory, and to develop the notion of securitization. For Wæver, securitization was dependent on the declaration by the political elites that an issue was a security problem, followed by the audience's acceptance that this declared security issue was indeed an important one that justified the application of extraordinary measures (Wæver, 1995). This acceptance of an issue being an existential threat is key to moving it from the area of 'normal politics' to the security arena. Following these ideas, securitization can be seen as a phenomenon resulting from social construction. Whether or not these issues are real threats is another debate. I will mostly focus on studying migration as a security threat following the practices of states in the current century. Because even though the perception of something as a threat is the result of a social construction, its application into practice is key for determining the 'success' of a securitization process. As the Paris School acknowledges through Bourdieu's work, linking agency and structure offers a comprehensive conception of practice positioning this in a structuralist constructivist work.[1] Therefore, this book will go beyond the understanding of securitization as a mere speech act and focus on the practices that have emerged as a result in the following chapters, mostly in the form of legal norms and policies.

The notion of securitization was originally defined as an existential framing of phenomena that takes place when there is an exception threat jeopardizing the survival of a referent object that legitimates the adoption of emergency measures to handle it instead of using ordinary democratic political processes (Wæver, 1995; Buzan et al., 1998). Securitization is thence the process of integrating non-security issues "into a security framework that emphasizes policing and defence" (Bourbeau, 2014), framed according to an exceptionalist rationality. In these cases, the use of extraordinary measures is

1 To read more on this, see the work of: Bourdieu, P. (1990). *The logic of practice*. Stanford Univeristy Press; Bourbeau, P. (2014). Moving forward together: Logics of the securitisation process. *Millennium: Journal of International Studies*, *43*(1), 187–206; Pouliot, V. (2008). The logic of practicality: A theory of practice of security communities. *International Organization*, *62*(2), 257–288.

justified, as these are presented as to protect from the particularly exceptional security threat.

There are different types of existential threats depending on the sector, including the military, political, environmental, or social sector. In the latter case, it is hard to establish boundaries that differentiate an existential threat to one that is not. The referent object in the social sector is collective identity, and identities have an evolving nature that makes it hard to distinguish if change comes from mere evolution or whether it comes from an external threat. Thus, it is relatively easy to start a securitization process, since many sources can be presented as an existential threat if adopting a more conservative, narrow-minded position. The arrival of migration, for instance, can be considered a threat to collective identity, or a mere phenomenon not affecting collective perception.

At the same time, it must be noted that the securitization logic is not always objectively justified, and an issue may be securitized not because of its nature or potential threat, but because it has been conferred this image by the political elite so that the audience perceives something as a danger from which it has to be protected. In other words, securitization is based on the intersubjective establishment of an existential threat (Roe, 2004), and this threat can be real, but sometimes it may not. Wæver (1995) goes as far as to argue that it is by calling an issue a threat, that it becomes one.

The approach taken by Balzacq (2005) on considering securitization from a strategic and pragmatic approach could give a wider picture of these securitization discourses. Other factors, such as the actor's capabilities, the position of the actor, the social identity, and the capacity to target the audience are also elements to consider when analyzing these discourses. This view also shows that securitization is largely based on power and the capacity to build something as a social and political threat (Taureck, 2006). These are factors which contribute to building a more powerful message, one that reaches securitization more successfully. This pragmatic approach to securitization shows that securitization is a strategic practice in which all its parts are relevant and affect the probability of success of the message being sent.

Therefore, this book is based on a broader understanding of securitization, one that encompasses both speech acts and practices, and as a result of these discourses offers a more comprehensive interpretation of the process. From this perspective, there is only securitization when these speech acts are turned into laws and/or policies that *de facto* bring migration to the security arena and produce some kind of social change. The speech act is not decisive by itself, but it is dependent on the consecutive actions that result from it.

However, the securitization of migration is not a new phenomenon, but an old one (Nagtegaal, 2011) as we find examples from decades ago, such as when Kurdish and Algerian diasporas were associated with terrorism in Western Europe during the 1970s and 1980s (Koser, 2011). However, what we have seen is after September 11 this phenomenon has appeared more forcefully in Western nations through the so-called War on Terror. Immigration was already associated with certain insecurities before 9/11, but the events of that day further legitimized the security rationale behind migration policy control that had prevailed in Europe since the 1970s (Chebel d'Appollonia, 2012). From the one hand, the terrorist attacks of 2001 created a clear situation of exceptionality which easily justified the application of an important number of security measures, including policies concerning immigration. From the other hand, the political elite deliberately connected issues related to migration to those related to terrorism so that the public fear on immigration exploits and is then able to transfer immigration out of the realms of conventional politics to the domain of emergency politics (Messina, 2014; Boswell, 2009).

Therefore, while different authors have continuously framed securitization practices within a new wave of securitization, I would like to argue that this follows mostly a Western vision of securitization. Security studies have thence "boomed" since the events of September 11 (Huysmans, 2014). The events of September 11 led to a clear extraordinary situation calling for the adoption of security measures to prevent further similar attacks from happening. And while this book analyzes securitization practices since the beginning of the century, 9/11 is not the sole defining landmark for this research. Let's pause for a moment to further clarify this. The terrorist events of 2001 on US soil turned into a new wave of securitization measures in the United States and other Western countries. After the terrorist attacks, the US developed a series of laws and security strategies – as will be seen in Chapter 5 – establishing a clear link between migration and security. With subsequent terrorist events in the European Union, the EU and its Member States continued developing counter-terrorist legislation targeting immigration. Even though these practices have been reinforced following non-terrorist events (such as with the case of the migratory crisis of 2015), this "new wave" of securitization of migration has as its landmark the events of 9/11 and the Global War on Terror. But that is mostly the case for Western nations. In non-Western states, I argue that these practices have been developed following different logics beyond that of countering the terrorist threat and they have been implemented partly as a response to Western practices which have expanded in the field but also following national interests not related to securitization in the West. To prove this point, the analysis of securitization practices of both Western and non-Western nations will be presented in Chapters 5 to 8. This will be useful to compare different laws and policies connecting migration to security in different nations and regions in the world, and it will also show that securitization follows different logics and justifications adapted to the social, economic, historic, and type of regime of the country being analyzed.

Security, migration, and morality

There are different questions arising in relation to the securitization of migration, regarding the ways in which the process takes place, the actors involved, and the referent objects that must be secured. Therefore, there are different perspectives from which to analyze securitization studies. A large section of migration studies focuses on the politicization of migration, which includes areas such as integration, welfare and social protection, citizenship, and discrimination (Brubaker, 1992; Geddes, 2003; Bello, 2017a; Lucarelli et al., 2020). This area has an important political but also social focus, as scholars seek to understand, for instance, what drives the mobilization of anti-immigrant sentiment or different political behaviors towards immigration. Another important scholarly section is that analyzing the consequences of the securitization practices on migration (Caloz-Tschopp, 2004; Freedman, 2004). Most attention is brought to highlighting the negative effects of securitization practices through humanitarian and human rights considerations, studying the implications of applying restrictive measures towards immigration in different countries. A different strand of migration studies centers the attention on how these measures are applied. In this case, scholars study the forms and practicalities of the securitization of migration to understand the mechanisms that facilitate securitization, the ways in which the process is carried out (Buzan et al., 1998; Bourbeau, 2011; Huysmans, 2014).

It is equally important to ask whether the securitization of migration is justified and morally right, as these practices have enormous consequences for the rights of these vulnerable groups. This book would like to argue that the securitization of migration is part of a large securitization pattern that is spread around the globe as a result of changes in the international order, as states are more commonly addressing both real and perceived threats as security risks. But to do so, it must firstly analyze the reasoning behind the securitization of migration to understand if this is a process that is necessary to contend a real threat or if it is the result of a growing interest by states to securitize areas that they want to control.

It is thus important to start with determining the moral rightness of securitization in the case of migration. Is it justified to securitize migration? Are those exceptional measures adopted to contend migration necessary to protect our societies? Or are securitization discourses used by the political elite to advance securitization measures that would otherwise be hard to implement? To establish the moral rightness of securitization, a key element to consider is the intent. As mentioned earlier, the Copenhagen School states that the political elite *deliberately* connects an issue such as migration to security. It is therefore crucial to determine whether decision makers act purposefully when linking migration to security. And then, whether this intentionality is justified because there is a real threat, or whether securitization has been used for purposes other than that of the protection of the referent object.

At times, securitization may be unavoidable to contend a particular security threat. But other times, it is the failure to deal with issues through normal politics that lies behind these actions. Or even the interest to avoid ordinary politics so that extraordinary measures that would otherwise be hard to implement are instead approved. Securitization is always a political choice (Buzan et al., 1998). The intent to securitize an issue is one of the elements that defines securitization. However, the moral rightness of these actions is not. But it is still important to differentiate between the two, since one is a justified process to defend the referent unit, and the other is merely a means to advance measures covered by false premises.

It is thus crucial to establish the moral rightness of securitization. For an issue to be resolved through the adoption of extraordinary measures there must be, first, an existential threat. A threat reaches this category when it compromises the survival of the referent object. There are many threats endangering an individual or social or political unit. But not all of them are existential. When we talk about securitization, there is a powerful actor claiming that an issue can be so hazardous as to destroy a particular unit. But these claims are not necessarily true.

It may sometimes be difficult to differentiate an objective existential threat from a perceived one. Floyd (2011) argues that what distinguishes the first from the latter is that in the first case, the aggressor really intends to attack a referent object, and that, at the same time, it has the means to do so. If the aggressor has both the intention and the capabilities to attack the referent object, it is much more likely that we are dealing with something more than a perceived threat, but a 'real' one. However, it seems that today we are also more often dealing with 'potential threats' than real ones (Bello, 2017a). These potential threats are characterized by their unpredictability. The clearest example is the terrorist threat, as it is almost impossible to predict when, where, or against whom an attack will be directed. And while years ago we were more used to seeing terrorism as a phenomenon taking place at the national level in countries like Spain, Ireland, or Italy, what we see today is that terrorism has gone beyond the national domain and has trespassed international barriers. One of the clearest examples of an international terrorist group causing great devastation is the Islamic State. These terrorist attacks are a real security threat. Nevertheless, they have also been used to securitize other areas, such as migration.

Thus, the qualification of something as a threat is not the only element to consider when determining when a securitization process is morally right. It is also important to see whether the response given to contend that threat is appropriate. The weight of the response should be proportional according to the strength of the threat. Therefore, it is in fact possible that the use of extraordinary measures is justified if that is what it takes to ensure the survival of the referent object. However, when the securitizing actor uses measures outside of the ordinary process, but these are not consistent with the potentiality of the threat and are instead used to advance measures that would otherwise be hard or impossible to apply, then securitization is unjustified and unrestrained by morality.

Most scholars agree that Western politicians engage in this kind of discourse linking migration to security for self-interested political reasons and/

or in order to increase and enhance the legitimacy of their privileged positions (Karyotis, 2007; Messina, 2014). There is thus an interest for those in power to securitize migration. The securitization discourse legitimizes the application of emergency measures and other non-conventional measures that in a normal situation would be hard to implement. And when the public widely accepts something as a security threat, these measures are accepted as necessary to combat the potential threat and to maintain the security of the nation. If no decisive action is taken, there is the risk of being destroyed. And because the protection of the political entity or society (depending on the threat) is of utmost priority, national defense cannot be overlooked. This paves the way for those in power to apply measures that would otherwise be hard to implement.

Furthermore, it also represents a chance for the political elite to reinforce collective identification and generate "greater loyalty and patriotism by defining a particular issue as a common threat" (Boswell, 2007), and this works particularly well with migration, since the "issue" we are referring to are peoples with different cultures and values, disconnected from the national identity. It is relatively easy then to divide society and separate those who do not meet a certain national identity from those nationals in the host country. Again, the identification of the 'other' is made, strengthening the perception that what is not identifiable with 'us' is the enemy. And it is through the mobilization of the imaginary of war and enemy construction that the struggle for survival becomes concrete and acute, building the securitization process.

Migration – and especially irregular migration – is often presented as the source of criminality, the vehicle for importing terrorists, or the reason why infectious diseases are spread throughout. And these ideas are continuously presented to the population. The securitization of migration has therefore been a response to different events such as massive refugee flows, the incapacity of Western countries to respond to incoming influxes, and the terrorist threat among others. The political elite has used this context to frame migration as a national security threat, and discourses linking migration to terrorism have not only proliferated but have also consolidated this security logic. And when something is linked to security, it can even lead to the violation of human rights to protect it (Bonet, 2022). The result of this process is that there is a separation between 'us' and 'them'. There is a division within the population that fosters a negative vision of the 'other', the migrant, who is a threat to society and from which we need to be protected. It is by establishing this divide that a sense of hostility is built within host countries towards immigration.

Dealing with migration across borders: the externalization of migration

Stephen Krasner (1999) talks about the state's "interdependence sovereignty" to refer to the ability that states must have to dictate who has the right to cross their borders. States have strong interests in controlling their borders for maintaining control over internal security, preventing external threats, controlling who is allowed to enter to one's territory, and a long etcetera. Border control is thence an important part of a state's sovereignty and a state's national security.

By the end of the 20th century, having the nation-state as a central element in international relations and considering sovereignty as the cornerstone to understanding state relations seemed to be part of a previous order, and the international community was now paving the way for a new century where territories would no longer be the main referent element. However, the importance of borders increased during the second half of the 1990s and specially after the September 11 events (Vallet & David, 2012). Thence it was not only due to the terrorist attacks of 2001 that this perception changed, but the hardening of borders was already taking place before 9/11. As explained by Bissonnette and Vallet (2021), "the hardening of old borders and the definition of new borders . . . is fed not by a specific fear of terrorism but rather by global insecurities bred by globalization". These authors argue that globalization generated a series of insecurities, and the need to preserve national identities became more evident to nation-states. Thus, instead of the eradication of borders in the new century, globalization made states more insecure, which in turn generated a new border symbolism. The September 11 attacks later reinforced this need to reinforce border structures. In fact, one of the immediate responses to these attacks by the United States government was to dedicate more control efforts along their southern border with Mexico. Although there was no evidence that the perpetrators of the attack had entered the country through these frontiers, fear and anxiety spread the logic that border enforcement were an important part of counter-terrorist strategies. Over time, these measures have only continued to grow.

The externalization of migration then refers to those extraterritorial state actions directed to prevent migrants, including asylum seekers, from entering the territory of a destination country or region, or making them legally inadmissible without assessing their cases individually (Frelick et al., 2016). Most of the times, these measures are presented through a humanitarian veil which explains that they are set to protect the lives of migrants who are at risk at sea or at the hands of smugglers. But they are also an effort to prevent irregular migration from reaching destination countries. Very often, part of these measures also includes agreements with third countries to address the "root causes" of migration. That is, they seek to help other countries develop rule of law and respect for human rights, so that their citizens do not feel the need to flee their homes. Through unilateral, bilateral, and multilateral initiatives, agreements and policies are presented as a way to refrain immigrants from embarking on boats and putting their lives at risk.

Border politics strongly rely on identity elements, differentiating between those who are citizens and thus part of the society, and those who are not, and therefore constructing a vision of the 'other'. Massive incoming migratory flows can overwhelm the state's capacity to control its borders or to provide public services, and they have further contributed to reinforcing this vision of the 'other'. As Adamson (2006) explains, in weak states, this can lead to conflicts over resources. In advanced industrial states, what we see is that the states establish higher formal control processes over migration, which results in higher numbers of organized criminal networks around illegal migration that are in competition, and in turn more dangerous journeys for these migrants to escape state control. She refers to this phenomenon as a "cat-and-mouse game between migration pressures and state control over borders". In this aspect, it is important to highlight the extraterritorial dimension of migration control, as state practices to control incoming migration before it even reaches one's land have proliferated in recent years. The way in which states are dealing with migration as a 'national threat' is not only an approach taken at the national level but is also externalized, and thus causing effects beyond their own borders.

Boswell (2003) also recognizes that Member States of the EU have exported migration control instruments such as those relating to border control, not only to the EU level, but further beyond. She gives different arguments to explain this. Firstly, these were exported to sending and transit countries, and secondly, future Member States were obliged to accept the Schengen *acquis* into their legislation (such as stricter border control and asylum policies). Another element of externalization comprises instruments facilitating the return of asylum seekers and illegal migrants to third countries, as well as other readmission agreements and provisions on safe third countries of transit. Thus securitization, as much as it has been debated, is in fact a phenomenon that is happening at the international arena and concerns states globally. Thence one of the ways to externalize migration and border control is the state's investment in new technologies to reinforce its border control. Large-scale biometric data systems to monitor those entering one's territory, drones to detect migrant boats at sea, and camera surveillance systems are just a few examples of sophisticated technologies implemented in the past years by states to control incoming population and refrain unwanted migration.

Western states have developed a wide range of mechanisms to control migratory flows, and the use of technology is just one of them. International cooperation in the field is not a new praxis; however, these have been intensified, and in a wide range of operations. For instance, while terrorism used to be considered a national security topic, now multilateral exchange has become key to tackling this threat. Practices on information-sharing were considered risky before, but as terrorist groups have evolved and internationalized, states have seen the necessity to address associated terrorist issues from a multilateral perspective. In this sense, information sharing has become a rather common practice and is now part of the solution to control international terrorists to avoid fragmented intelligence data across services

(Andreeva, 2021). However, the goal of this inter-state cooperation is also to assist other countries with migration management so that they are the ones to prevent these peoples from migration to other countries.

The reinforcement of security agencies such as the European Agency for the Management of Operational Cooperation at the External Borders (Frontex) in the case of the European Union is an important example to show the strength of these units in relation to border control and border externalization. The agency was established by Council Regulation EC 2007/2004 of 26 October 2004 to enhance security at the external borders of EU Member States and fight cross-border crimes. In its beginnings Frontex helped Member States respond to certain 'migration crises', as with the case of the 2005–2006 'migration crisis' at the Spanish external borders (Léonard & Kaunert, 2022), or the 2015–2016 'migration crisis' affecting mostly southern EU Member States in the Mediterranean. In the latter case, for instance, Frontex initiated operations Triton and Poseidon to support Greece and Italy, focusing on border control, surveillance and search and rescue activities (Cusumano, 2019). But Frontex also started cooperating with other actors with more important military means such as the North Atlantic Treaty Organization (NATO) to "tackle the refugee and migrant crisis".[2] Over time, Frontex has improved and advanced its technological capacities and increased in personnel, while developing maritime operations, cooperating with both states and non-state actors such as NATO and Europol. Again, these practices and the growing importance of security agencies in the field of both border and migration control show the existing continuum between migration and security, a connection that has widely surpassed international borders.

Border externalization and securitization have now been in place for many years. In 1992, Morocco and Spain signed a readmission agreement by which Morocco agreed to readmit deportees returned from Spain. Today, the instrument can be mentioned as a mere example of an externalization measure through a readmission agreement. And these types of agreements have become a cornerstone of the migratory policy of the European Union (Walia, 2021). More recently, these dynamics have moved towards the development of national security strategies. They may have an international reach, but they are designed at the national level and considering the national security preferences of the country. Frontex may be an international agency fostering the securitization of migration, but many other externalization measures are also taken nationally.

Monar (2015) has written in this regard. He argues that in the European Union, there can be collective actions taken when there is a common threat

2 In the words of the same *North Atlantic Treaty Organisation in the 'NATO's Deployment in the Aegean Sea', Fact Sheet, of October 2016. Brussels:* NATO. *Public Diplomacy Division – Press & Media Section.*

that needs of a response resulting from a complex decision-making procedure that usually also requires an important mobilization of financial resources. The 9/11 attacks created this common threat perception within the EU. Furthermore, at the time the terrorist threat was presented as a threat to democratic societies, and a global coalition was needed to protect the international community. In the following months, the EU responded with a common international counter-terrorist action including both internal and external measures. It emerged as an important cooperation partner for agreements on counter-terrorism and has been a capable international actor in the field. However, Member States have retained control over counter-terrorist action, as operational counter-terrorism capabilities have remained at their hands. And in the past years they have strengthened this national vision of security, prioritizing the adoption of security strategies from a national perspective, moving away from international cooperation. As he observes:

> The new threat perception and international collective action needs after the 9/11 attacks have presented the EU with an "opportunity" to assume new roles and responsibilities in a field in which it had before legally none and practically hardly any. This opportunity has clearly been used, although the Member States – given the national security sensitivity of the field – have kept the EU's role under tight control and constraints.
>
> (Monar, 2015)

What this shows is that the securitization of migration, and the externalization of migration, have remained at the hands of the state. The Global War on Terror was depicted as an international threat, but the state still considers it of utmost importance to maintain its control over migration and security. And while today even those measures adopted nationally may have an international reach, these are nevertheless still designed at the domestic level and following national interests. In a world shaped by globalization, sovereignty on migratory issues still follows the traditional view of state power.

Migration and terrorism: a revision of national sovereignty

Some scholars point at the multilateral response given to the terrorist threat following collective securitization (Haacke & Williams, 2008; Sperling & Webber, 2017, 2019; Kaunert & Léonard, 2019; Shepherd, 2021). According to Haacke and Williams (2008), collective securitization is the process by which "one or more securitizing actors within a (regional) arrangement identify(ies) a particular development or issue as an existential threat to a security referent". The authors argue that NATO has collectively securitized its response to the Russian actions in Ukraine, well before the start of the invasion of 2022. Also following this collective securitization theory, other authors have argued that since the events of 9/11, the European Union and its Member States have collectively securitized terrorism. Terrorism has led many states to design counter-terrorist policies. They have treated terrorism as a transboundary security threat requiring a response that overcomes the traditional separation between internal and external security (Kaunert & Léonard, 2019; Shepherd, 2021). This has also been covered in the previous sections with examples on the externalization of migration, and this breach between internal and external affairs, where national decisions lead to effects trespassing boundaries.

But there are also other theories such as that of Buzan and Wæver (2009), who use the concept of *macrosecuritizations* to refer to those referent objects higher than those at the middle level and which have a wider international scope. Macrosecuritizations put together multiple lower-level securitizations and identify a common existential threat that needs an exceptional measure to respond to it. These securitizations are placed above the state and national level, and they put together lower-level security issues within the larger framework, consolidating them as global threats to security. Due to their nature, any reaction will have to compromise liberal values and will be considered securitization, but these actions are justified since they are widely accepted as global security threats affecting civilization. An example of macrosecuritization would be the US projection of the Global War on Terror and the events following 9/11, as the country always defended that this became a global threat to civilization and international security.[3] In this sense, the US was successful in claiming that its allies had to decide whether they wanted to be with them in this War on Terror, or against them. Securitization discourses are discourses of unity (Von Rosen, 2019), as they define the 'other' as a threat to what is 'us' (Buonfino, 2004). But securitization also serves political interests by sustaining and strengthening power relations (Laclau, 2001). In this sense, the US was successful in its approach to introduce its allies in the war against terrorism. The Global War on Terror presented terrorism as a threat to international security, but it was also about the protection of the existing liberal order. As explained by Buzan and Wæver (2009):

> Partly it was about existing order universalism and the threat posed by violent non-state actors to the institutions of sovereignty, territoriality, diplomacy and the interstate order generally. And partly it was about

3 For further discussion on this subject see: Buzan, B. (2004). *The United States and the great powers: World politics in the twenty-first century*. Polity; Buzan, B. (2006). Will the 'global war on terrorism' be the new Cold War? *International Affairs*, *82*(6); Buzan, B., & Waever, O. (2009). Macrosecuritisation and security constellations: Reconsidering scale in securitisation theory. *Review of International Studies*, *35*, 253–276; Buzan, B., Waever, O., & Wilde, J. (1998). *Security: A new framework for analysis*. Lynne Reinner.

> physical threat universalism as embodied in the linkage of terrorists to weapons of mass destruction.
>
> (Buzan and Wæver, 2009)

Nevertheless, the terrorist threat which led to a US-led response with the support of its allies started losing weight over time and gave way to measures focused mostly on migration. At first, migration was strongly linked to the terrorist threat. Refugee flows were presented as the ways through which terrorists arrived camouflaged. Measures to contend incoming migration, to reinforce borders and increase internal controls of peoples with a particular ethnic profile increased and became rather common in a wide range of countries. After each terrorist attack, some political and media discourses put the focus on the migrant population. And in times of economic recession, immigrants were again pointed at as one of the reasons why the welfare system was incapable of coping with national needs. In time, the terrorist threat was just one of the threats associated with migration, but there were many other arguments presented against the migrant population. This in turn led to bringing the 'international threat' of migration to the hands of national security. More measures were designed by states to contend migratory flows, and the management of migration as a national security threat became more evident. And while migration is still an international phenomenon, in recent years it has been more commonly managed through domestic politics.

Territorial frontiers are one of the main elements defining state sovereignty, and border control is thus one of the most crucial areas of state management. As border control and migration control go hand in hand, migration has always been dealt with at the national level. Decisions on who is allowed to enter one's territory is a matter of a state's control. Migration law regulates passports, visas, nationality, residence, employment authorizations, and expelling foreigners, among other related issues. These are standards deriving from state sovereignty. The nation state is thus a legitimator of law (Hirst & Thompson, 1996). Or as put by Dauvergne (2003), "the current era therefore re-emphasizes the pairing of sovereignty and migration, and in the process brings questions of migration closer to the core of rule of law ideology." It is in this way that migration law, border control, and sovereignty have outweighed international cooperation and have brought migration to the national security domain, once again. Von Rosen explains how the securitization of migration has been used in recent years to reinforce national security strategies:

> The securitization of migration, however, has an additional political advantage: It is a welcome chance for states to reinforce the concept of national sovereignty, which in the past decades has been weakened by new developments in the sphere of international public law, particularly the idea of transnationally applicable, universal human rights. In its core meaning, sovereignty describes a government's supreme authority within

> a territory and over a specific group of people (the nation's citizens). This authority goes hand in hand with a set of self-imposed obligations that the modern sovereign state owes to its citizens (but not all of them to non-citizens), such as a certain level of security, welfare provisions, rights and freedoms. Beyond these obligations, however, the sovereign state may in principle act at will, as long as the effects are limited to its own territory and people.
>
> (Von Rosen, 2019)

Migration is thus seen as a threat to the sovereignty of states, pluralism and globalization are a danger to the unity of the community, and the result leads to the adoption of national security measures further controlling migration. However, it is important to note that political and media discourses on the unity of the community and protecting the nation against external threats may lead to the abuse of national security instruments for immediate political goals. If those in power continue legislating and using public policies to contend the so-called migration threat, the result will be no other than the weakening of the rule of law.

Conclusion

Human migration may be an age-old activity, but migration movements have evolved and changed in the past years, and they are shaped by both historical and recent events. In 1970, migrants represented 2.3% of the global population. In 2020, the estimate was at 3.6% (IOM, 2022). Some are leaving their homes to work or study, searching for better opportunities. Many others are fleeing their countries escaping from conflict, persecution, or environmental disaster.

These movements of people have provoked worldwide concern and uncertainty. The presentation of migration – and particularly irregular migration – as a "security problem" has been normalized (Huysmans, 2000, 2006). As explained in Chapter 3, the nature of the perceived threat can change according to the time and place, and the context of the country. And while migration has been considered a social and economic phenomenon, today it is also seen as a security threat, and it is an important part of global debates. The securitization of migration has now become rather common. Political ideas, media discourses, laws, and policies have all generated a continuous progression that has resulted in the never-ending process to securitize migration.

There are two approaches from which scholars and practitioners can see migration. From a liberal approach, migration is seen from a humanitarian perspective, considering the human rights of individuals, and seeking to ensure their protection. Or from a realist policy frame, migration is seen as a threat to national security, and it is thus justified to apply restrictive measures to increase border control and contend immigration. The selection of one security frame or another is extremely important, as this will be the standard way to define an issue within the security framework and therefore create laws and policies accordingly. It would be fair to say that in the past years the securitization of migration has followed a realist approach that has driven states to treat migration as a security threat at the expense of human rights and humanitarian considerations.

What is more, while the response to the attacks of September 11 had an important international reach, security issues – and especially those concerning migration – have remained mostly within the domestic sphere. And as a new wave of securitization measures began after the events of 2001, these practices are most often adopted at the national stage. States may still cooperate with one another in security-related issues, but they have maintained a preference to deal with security threats from a national standpoint. And while today's world may bring more global security threats, such as those concerning migration movements or the climate change, national security is always foregoing. As a result, securitization has become common practice, and in the field of migration this has remained mostly a national security matter.

The next chapters seek to show precisely that the securitization of migration has advanced mostly through the design and application of domestic laws and policies. In the following pages, the measures of different states around the world will be used to depict the progression of securitization measures in the field of migration since the events of September 11. The cases that have been selected are relevant from a migration perspective because they deal with important migration figures, mostly in the form of incoming migratory flows. It is thence interesting to study how these states deal with foreigners and what measures – in the policy and legal field – have been adopted to manage immigration. As will be shown, in most cases, there is an important nexus connecting immigration to security, even though this is justified for different reasons and depending on each state's social, economic, or historical context. The wider picture shows that the securitization of migration has taken place in states of different regions around the world, showing that since the events of September 11, there has been a spillover effect leading to a generalized process of diffusion of securitization practices in this area. Securitization is not only a phenomenon of Western countries and consequence of the Global War on Terror. It is an international phenomenon that has been spread around the world and justified following different "insecurity rationales". The aim of the study of these cases is to show that a realist vision of security remains. And that if the values, liberties, and the human rights that the liberal order has tried to promote for so long are to be maintained, action to protect the rights of the most vulnerable must be taken.

References

Adamson, F. (2006). Crossing borders: International migration and national security. *International Security*, *31*(1), 165–199.

Andreeva, C. (2021). The evolution of information-sharing in EU counter-terrorism post-2015: A paradigm shift? *Global Affairs*, *7*(5), 751–776.

Balzacq, T. (2005). The three faces of securitization: Political agency, audience and context. *European Journal of International Relations*, *11*(2).

Bello, V. (2017a). *International migration and international security: Why prejudice is a global security threat*. Routledge.

Bigo, D. (2002). Security and immigration: Toward a critique of the governmentality of unease. *Alternatives*, *27*, 63–92.

Bigo, D. (2008). Globalized (in)security. The field and the ban-opticon. In D. Bigo & A. Tsoukala (Eds.), *Terror, insecurity, and liberty* (pp. 10–49). Routledge.

Bissonnette, A., & Vallet, É. (2021). *Borders and border walls. In-security, symbolism, vulnerabilities*. Routledge.

Bonet, J. (2022). La pobreza como vector de inseguridad global e interna: una aproximación regulatoria. *Revista de Estudios en Seguridad Internacional*, *8*(2), 1–21.

Boswell, C. (2003). The 'external dimension' of EU immigration and asylum policy. *International Affairs*, *79*(3), 619–638.

Boswell, C. (2007). Migration control in Europe after 9/11: Explaining the absence of securitisation. *Journal of Common Market Studies*, *45*(3), 589–610.

Boswell, C. (2009). Migration, security and legitimacy: Some reflections. In T. Givens, G. P. Freeman, & D. L. Leal (Eds.), *Immigration policy and security: U.S., European, and commonwealth perspectives*. Routledge.

Bourbeau, P. (2011). *The securitization of migration. A study of movement and order*. Routledge.

Bourbeau, P. (2014). Migration, exceptionalist security discourse, and practices. In *Handbook on migration and security*. Edward Elgar Press.

Brubaker, R. (1992). *Citizenship and nationhood in France and Germany*. Harvard University Press.

Buonfino, A. (2004). Between unity and plurality: The politicization and securitization of the discourse of immigration in Europe. *New Political Science*, *26*(1), 23–49.

Buzan, B., & Wæver, O. (2009). Macrosecuritisation and security constellations: Reconsidering scale in securitisation theory. *Review of International Studies*, *35*, 253–276.

Buzan, B., Wæver, O., & de Wilde, J. (1998). *Security: A new framework for analysis*. Lyne Rienner Publishers.

Caloz-Tschopp, M. C. (2004). *Les étrangers aux frontières de l'Europe et le spectre des camps*. La Dispute.

Chebel d'Appollonia, A. (2012). *Frontiers of fear: Immigration and insecurity in the United States and Europe*. Cornell University Press.

Cusumano, E. (2019). Migrant rescue as organized hypocrisy: EU maritime missions offshore Libya between humanitarianism and border control. *Cooperation and Conflict*, *54*(1), 3–24.

Dauvergne, C. (2003). *Challenges to sovereignty: Migration laws for the 21st Century* (Working Paper No. 92). United Nations High Commissioner for Refugees, New Issues in Refugee Research.

Floyd, R. (2011). Can securitization theory be used in normative analysis? Towards a just securitization theory. *Security Dialogue*, *42*(4–5), 427–439.

Freedman, J. (2004). *Immigration and insecurity in France*. Routledge.

Frelick, B., Kysel, I., & Podkul, J. (2016). The impact of externalization of migration controls on the rights of asylum seekers and other migrants. *Journal of Migration and Human Security*, *4*(4), 190–220.

Geddes, A. (2003). *The politics of migration and immigration in Europe*. Sage.

Haacke, J., & Williams, P. (2008). Regional arrangements, securitization, and transnational security challenges: The African Union and the Association of Southeast Asian Nations compared. *Security Studies*, *17*(4), 775–809.

Hirst, P., & Thompson, G. (1996). *Globalization in question*. Polity Press.

Huntington, S. P. (2004, March/April). The Hispanic challenge. *Foreign Policy*, 30–45.

Huysmans, J. (2000). The European Union and the securitization of migration. *Journal of Common Market Studies*, *38*(5), 751–777.

Huysmans, J. (2006). *The politics of insecurity*. Routledge.

Huysmans, J. (2014). *Security unbound. Enacting democratic limits*. Routledge.

Huysmans, J., & Squire, V. (2017). Migration and security. In M. Dunn Cavelty & T. Balzacq (Eds.), *Routledge handbook of security studies* (2nd ed.). Routledge.

IOM. (2022). World migration report 2022. *International Organization for Migration*. Retrieved October 23, 2023, from https://publications.iom.int/system/files/pdf/WMR-2022.pdf

Karyotis, G. (2007). European migration policy in the aftermath of September 11: The security-migration nexus. *Innovation: The European Journal of Social Science Research*, *20*(1), 1–17.

Kaunert, C., & Léonard, S. (2019). The collective securitisation of terrorism in the European Union. *West European Politics*, *42*(2), 261–277.

Koser, K. (2011). When is migration a security issue? *Brookings*. Retrieved July 10, 2023, from www.brookings.edu/articles/when-is-migration-a-security-issue/

Krasner, S. (1999). *Sovereignty: Organized hypocrisy*. Princeton University Press.

Laclau, E. (2001). Democracy and the Question of Power. *Constellations, 8*(1), 3–14.

Léonard, S., & Kaunert, C. (2022). The securitisation of migration in the European Union: Frontex and its evolving security practices. *Journal of Ethnic and Migration Studies*, *48*(6), 1417–1429.

Lucarelli, S., Sperling, J., & Webber, M. (2020). *Collective securitisation and security governance in the European Union*. Routledge.

Messina, A. (2014). Securitizing immigration in the age of terror. *World Politics*, *66*(3), 530–559.

Monar, J. (2015). The EU as an international counter-terrorism actor: Progress and constraints. *Intelligence and National Security*, *30*(2), 333–356.

Nagtegaal, K. (2011). Security, insecurity and refugees in the Netherlands. In G. Lazaridis (Ed.), *Security, insecurity and migration in Europe*. Routledge.

Roe, P. (2004). Securitization and minority rights: Conditions of desecuritization. *Security Dialogue*, *35*(3), 279–294.

Rudolph, C. (2003). Security and the political economy of international migration. *American Political Science Review*, *97*(4), 603–620.

Shepherd, A. (2021). EU counterterrorism, collective securitization, and the internal-external security nexus. *Global Affairs*, *7*(5), 733–749.

Sperling, J., & Webber, M. (2017). NATO and the Ukraine crisis: Collective securitisation. *European Journal of International Security*, *2*(1), 19–46.

Sperling, J., & Webber, M. (2019). The European Union: Security governance and collective securitisation. *West European Politics*, 42(2), pp. 228–260.

Taureck, R. (2006). Securitization theory and securitization studies. *Journal of International Relations and Development*, 9, 53–61.

Vallet, É., & David, C.-P. (2012). Introduction: The (re)building of the wall in international relations. *Journal of Borderlands Studies*, 27(2), 111–119.

Von Rosen, J. (2019). The securitization of migration as a threat to liberal, democratic societies. *Security and Peace*, 37(1).

Wæver, O. (1995). Securitization and desecuritization. In R. D. Lipshutz (Ed.), *On security* (pp. 46–86). Columbia University Press.

Walia, H. (2021). *Border and rule: Global migration, capitalism and the rise of racist nationalism*. Haymarket Books.

Part 2

Regional case studies

5

Securitizing migration in the Americas

Migration in the American region: the cases of the United States and Mexico

The United States has been the main country of destination for international migrants since the 1970s, while Mexico is the second-largest country of origin (IOM, 2022). The Mexico-US corridor is one of the most heavily travelled. That is the reason why these two countries within the American continent have been selected. The case of the United States will be used to show if and what kind of securitization measures have been applied in the context of an important destination country. At the same time, and as has been manifested, a new securitization wave started after the events of September 11. Since this is the country where those events took place, it will also be particularly insightful to identify the evolution of such measures in the context of the terrorist threat.

On the other hand, Mexico does not only have citizens emigrating to its northern neighboring country, but it is also an important transit country for Latin Americans trying to reach US soil. The Central American Route is used by millions of Latin Americans who are trying to move to the United States. And while there are many Mexicans trying to cross the northern border, there are also many others coming from Central America, making their treacherous journeys through smuggling routes, escaping from poverty and violence. The case of Mexico will therefore be a useful example as it is a country which has transitioned from being mostly of origin and transit, to also being one of destination. This complexity has shaped security policies in the past years, but it is now also introducing securitization measures both to contend immigration flows and a pressing US government.

The case of the United States of America

The United States is a nation whose measures on the field of security have been more than often questioned. The country has invested in border control and security technologies in the past decades, and with even more intensity after the events of 9/11. By establishing barriers at the border, allocating funds for electronic surveillance, and augmenting the number of personnel

DOI: 10.4324/9781003458159-7

at border stations, the US has tried to reinforce its security policies to refrain migrants from entering the country (Cinoglu & Atun, 2013; Migration Policy Institute, 2001).

After the 9/11 attacks, some called for severe restrictions on immigration and anti-immigrant forces took advantage of the security rhetoric. The US government responded to the attacks in the same way it has in so many other times in history, that is, by using national security as a justification for incarcerating and deporting immigrants in a wave designed to defend the nation (Ewing et al., 2015). Many scholars agree that the attacks became a major turning point in the way immigration was dealt with in the country. Since that moment on, "immigration and terrorism became inextricably linked in the US public debate on security" (Kerwin, 2005).

The promptest reaction of the US government after the 9/11 attacks was the adoption of the USA Patriot Act. Passed less than six weeks after the attacks, it expanded the executive powers to fight the terrorist threat. Only 11 days after the September attack, Tom Ridge was appointed as the first Director of the Office of Homeland Security in the White House. This office became the Department of Homeland Security (DHS) about a year later, in December 2002. The creation of the department was a clear consequence of the terrorist attacks, and it represented an important sign of where the direction of migration management would be going from then on. Immigration was placed within the heart of the national security agenda, a link that has remained ever since (Waslin, 2009).

Focusing firstly on the USA PATRIOT Act, the piece defended the need for expanding the definition of terrorism and the range of aliens who could be deported from US territory on terrorism-related grounds, while also reducing their procedural rights. Overall, the migrant is very much at the center of this statute, being directly tackled and connected with terrorist offences. There were also more laws enacted in the field of both migration and terrorism. The Immigration and Nationality Act allowed the detention of aliens for 48 hours without charge, and this period could be enlarged if there were any "extraordinary circumstances" (Chebel d'Appollonia, 2012). The Uniting and Strengthening America by Providing Appropriate Tools Required to Intercept and Obstruct Terrorism (more commonly referred to as the USA Patriot Act or PATRIOT Act) is the first and more well-known example of this. Signed by George W. Bush on October 26, 2001, it gave law enforcement agencies the competence to investigate and bring terrorists to justice. This Act has been highly disputed as the definition of people carrying terrorist activities is so wide that it could include an extensive range of individuals. According to Dück and Lucke (2019)

> this anti-terror legislative package included measures to restrict civil liberties, introduce additional surveillance, increase border controls, as well as measures for a widely increased authority for intelligence agencies. . . . It

also enabled the US to detain suspects of terrorism without due process at the US military's Guantanamo Bay camp.

Several measures were adopted after 9/11 and other legislation and policies have been applied ever since. As put by Miller (2005), the USA Patriot Act 2001, the Homeland Security Act of 2002, and the Enhanced Border Security and Visa Entry Reform Act of 2002, collectively "illustrate the accelerating criminalization of the immigration system". But what is also interesting in this sense is the fact that the Bush administration categorized terrorist attacks as acts of war after the New York attacks in 2001. This is an important step, because during times of war the primary goal is to combat the enemy, and thus anti-terrorism measures shifted from the civilian to the military sphere (Dück & Lucke, 2019).

In 2002, the National Security Entry-Exit Registration System (NSEERS) was expanded, and it required male nationals from Arab and Muslim-majority countries such as Iran, Iraq, Libya, Sudan, and Syria admitted before 9/11 to report to an immigration office and register with the Immigration and Naturalization Service (INS). They were interviewed, were photographed, and got their fingerprints taken. Those who did not obey could be considered out of status and sent back to their countries. About 84,000 registered through this process and more than 13,000 men who complied with the registrations were placed in removal proceedings (AAI-USA, 2016).

After September 11, racial profiling became a recurrent tool to identify potential terrorists in the country. As Vandenberg (2004) explains, the long history of racism in the United States can result in viewing as enemies those members of minorities or immigrant origin, and "by permitting racial profiling to be an acceptable practice, noncitizens will be treated more like criminals and the rights of every U.S. citizen will subsequently decrease". And the fact that the perpetrators of the attacks were Arab male immigrants has led many to believe that it is necessary to pay closer attention to Arab-looking men (Cole, 2002). Proof of this view is that after 9/11, more than 1,200 noncitizens – mostly of Arab and South Asian origin – were apprehended (Taylor, 2002; Vandenberg, 2004). And later, in early 2002, the Department of Justice announced the apprehension and removal of 4,000 to 6,000 men of Arab countries such as Iraq, Iran, Libya, Sudan, Syria, Qatar, Somalia, Tunisia, Yemen, and Pakistan, among others (Vandenberg, 2004). Thence as Taylor (2004) affirms, "The arrest of hundreds of young men with Middle Eastern backgrounds has come to symbolize the fears within immigrant communities in the United States that current immigration enforcement policies are a product of federal discrimination", which raises serious questions on the protection of the rights of non-citizens of these origins, which may be sacrificed in exchange for ensuring the security concerns of the majority of the population.

As the United Nations Special Rapporteur on the human rights of migrants noted, back xenophobia and racism towards the immigrant population worsened after September 11, causing

> a particularly discriminatory and devastating impact on many of the most vulnerable groups in the migrant population, including children, unaccompanied minors, Haitian and other Afro-Caribbean migrants, and migrants who are, or are perceived to be, Muslim or of South Asian or Middle Eastern descent.
>
> (Bustamante, 2008)

In 2003, the Clear Law Enforcement for Criminal Alien Removal Act (CLEAR) was enacted. The law gave local police officers the power to enforce criminal and civil federal immigration laws. It also allowed for criminalization of all immigration violations and their registration into the National Crime Information Center (NCIC) database. Human Rights Watch warned that this law would lead to arbitrary arrests, deprivations of property and deportations, which could even involve the deportation of refugees who enter the country without valid documentation to a place where they might face persecution and thence breaching the principle of non-refoulement (Parker & Patten, 2004). The provisions of the Act fully authorize not only state officials, but also those at the local level to remove aliens in the country. More alarmingly, they would not even have to follow the procedures and checks usually required by the federal system, thus giving them with an extraordinary power that may lead to violations of basic rights.

The REAL ID Act of 2005 suggested increasing security levels by denying driver's licenses to illegal immigrants. Operation Return to Sender, a program led by Immigration and Customs Enforcement consisted in conducting raids to look for dangerous immigrant fugitives and terrorists. The cost for filing naturalization applications increased by 80% in 2007, following an unprecedented number of applications seeking to vote in the elections of the following year. Adversities have been established in all sorts of ways for immigrants, including refugees, in the United States. They have had to cope with difficulties not only to seek for a safe haven, but also to remain safe within it.

In 2014, as a response to the arrival of an increased number of unaccompanied Central Americans, the Department of Homeland Security launched "Operation Coyote", which involved information-sharing on criminal intelligence to prevent human smuggling and trafficking. This is another practice on border externalization, as it was destined to prevent migration leaving from Mexico in an attempt to stop it before reaching US borders. Over time, there has also been an important funding from the US to Mexico to reinforce the latter's southern border and prevent further crossings. The Mérida Initiative is one of such measures. This is a bilateral partnership which started in 2007 between the two countries and which has increased in funding over the years.

One of the pillars of the deal is to "create a 21st century US-Mexican border", focusing on preventing illegal migration and cross-border crime through the improvement of immigration enforcement (Ribando & Finklea, 2017).

These efforts to refrain immigration from the US-Mexico border have also been further reinforced with other Central American countries. In 2014, Honduran law enforcement units received funding from the United States to intercept children and families attempting to cross the border from Honduras into Guatemala (Frelick et al., 2016). In 2019 alone, the United States signed 11 bilateral agreements with Guatemala, Honduras, and El Salvador. These included 'Asylum Cooperative Agreements', 'Border Security Arrangements', 'Biometric Data Sharing Program Arrangements', and 'Temporary Agricultural and Non-agricultural Workers Programs Agreements'. As stated by the Department of Homeland Security, 72% of all migrants apprehended at the Southwest border were coming from these countries, which showed the necessity to enter into agreements and arrangements with each of these countries to solve the "causes of irregular migration" (Homeland Security, 2019a).

But there have been other measures taken more recently, such as the executive orders by President Trump to control immigration and connect it to national security. On January 25, 2017, only five days after being sworn in as president of the United States, he also issued two executive orders reinforcing the already existing process of securitization of migration in the country. With the Executive Order 13767 on Border Immigration Enforcement and with the Executive Order 13768 on Enhancing Public Safety in the Interior of the United States, the president approved building a massive wall between the US-Mexico border in addition to other proposals which undermined the basic rights of due process and the basic rights of those seeking asylum in the United States. The first of these instruments contended that the wall had to be built immediately and had to be monitored and supported by adequate personnel "so as to prevent illegal immigration, drug and human trafficking, and acts of terrorism" – Section 2(a). Other reasons given in the subsequent sections include to detain individuals who are suspected of committing federal or state law – Section 2(b) – or to remove individuals whose claims to stay in the US have been rejected – Section 2(d).

Two days later, Executive Order 13780 of March 6 also known as the "Executive Order Protecting the Nation From Foreign Terrorist Entry Into the United States" was also implemented. This addressed particularly banning entrance of foreigners from six Muslim countries (Chad, Iran, Libya, Syria, Yemen, and Somalia) to protect national security. Furthermore, Section 1 contends that the United States Refugee Admissions Program (USRAP) plays "a crucial role in detecting foreign nationals who may commit, aid, or support acts of terrorism". Again, the idea that terrorists may come hidden in refugee flows is manifested.

The Department of Homeland Security Appropriations Act of 2018 became the largest border enforcement and immigration budget in history

(Walia, 2021). In 2019, there was a record of 69,550 migrant children being incarcerated in the US, which was at the same time the highest number of children separated from their families and detained than in any other country on the planet (Al Jazeera, 2019). And for the first time in history, the Department of Homeland Security had to admit that "white nationalism and other far-right-wing extremists are the most significant domestic terrorism threats facing the United States" (Congress, 2019).

In recent years, President Joe Biden has taken different steps from his predecessor. On his first day in office in 2021, the US Citizenship Act was presented as a law to provide a pathway to US citizenship to about 11 million undocumented immigrants living in the country. The bill was also designed to authorize budget allocations for immigration enforcement to develop and implement a plan to deploy technology to expedite screening at the borders and training of border officers (The White House, 2021).

In addition, in 2023 the Dignity Act was passed in a bipartisan effort to address immigration reforms from different aspects. From the one hand, the 'Dignity Program' becomes an application process by which certain undocumented people who have been in the country for more than five years can apply to some authorizations. From the other hand, it is also strongly directed towards reinforcing national security. A budget of $35 billion is directed to enhancing and improving infrastructure and technology at the border to strengthen national security. In addition, it mandates a 60-day deadline for asylum seekers to make their claims and seeks to resolve most of these at the border via an asylum officer while preventing the release of these individuals while they wait for a decision on their claim in "humanitarian campuses". It also expands the grounds for inadmissibility and deportability, and the use of mandatory detention (AILA, 2023). The future political scenario will determine the extent of new measures securitizing migration, but nothing points towards migration leaving the security realm any time soon. In sum, while it is true that with the presidency of Joe Biden the design of migratory measures has shifted from the line of the previous president, migration and security are still strongly interconnected in the United States.

The case of Mexico

Mexico has been a transit country for a long time, but in the past years it has also been increasingly seen as a destination one, including for those who need international protection. The number of immigrants arriving in Mexico has increased more than 120% over the last two decades (UN DESA, 2020), and the number began drastically intensifying in 2018 (UNHCR, 2023). This is mostly due to growing violence, poverty, and unemployment in Central American countries. However, sudden climate events such as hurricanes have also been the cause of these moves going to Mexico and the United States in more recent years (Johns et al., 2023).

Herrera-Lasso and Artola (2011) analyze the consequences of 9/11 on immigration in Mexico. They argue that even though there should not have been any link between undocumented migration and national security, the events of September 11 changed this perception and derived in a series of changes in national legislation to increase control for certain types of incoming immigration. For instance, since 2008, entering Mexico without valid documentation is a criminal offence instead of an administrative fault, which used to be the case until then, according to the Ley General de Población (General Population Act). The authors compare new Mexican legislation with the terrorist attacks of 9/11, and those in Madrid in 2005 and London in 2007, where none of the terrorists were undocumented migrants. In fact, they were citizens of these countries or foreigners with legal documentation to travel. Nevertheless, terrorist attacks were associated with immigration, and new measures were adopted to further control incoming migration or obstruct their arrival and stay in the destination country. This connection between migration and security in Mexico was again raised by the former IOM Chief of Mission in Mexico, who explained that "the links between migration and security in Mexico, and particularly in border areas, have been growing since the events of September 11, 2001" (Artola, 2009).

The consequences of the attacks were thus not only seen in the worsening ways in which people's perception towards immigration changed, but these were also reflected in border management. There were major geostrategic changes in cooperation relations for border control between the United States, Mexico, and Guatemala (Ribando & Finklea, 2017). Mexico decided to develop a new border and immigration policy with its southern neighbors, and it has gradually strengthened border control since (Ramos-García et al., 2020). The "Plan Sur" was the first of these programs directed towards tackling irregular migration and it was approved under the mandate of President Vicente Fox. The program ran from 2001 to 2003, and it was one of the first responses to the events of September 11 by the Mexican government. Again, the fact that one of the first security measures adopted as a response to the terrorist attacks was one in relation to contending immigration shows the willingness to connect migration to security issues.

Other measures at the time include the Smart Border agreements signed between the United States with Canada and Mexico. In the agreement between the United States and Mexico signed in 2002, the goal was to secure borders and establish a common border infrastructure and border management system to "protect the citizens of both nations from terrorist, illegal drugs, and other dangers; facilitate and expedite legitimate cross border travel and commerce; and allow our governments to determine who crosses the borders" (The White House, 2002). Operation Centinela was another measure taken by Mexico in 2003 directed to strengthening detention operations of unauthorized immigrants and to fighting human trafficking.

Even though Mexico has been party to the 1951 Refugee Convention, its 1967 Protocol, and has signed the 1984 Cartagena Declaration, it was not until 2011 that the country finally adopted legislation in relation to refugees and asylum seekers through the Law on Refuges, Complementary Protection, and Political Asylum. The law was amended in 2014 and 2016 to expand the protections given to these groups and give them access to documentation that allows them to access employment, health care, and education. The latter reform granted them all the rights offered to Mexican citizens by the national constitution.

But as Mexico was increasing refugee protection nationally, it was also fortifying and strengthening border control. At the southern border it was doing so through *Programa Fontera Sur* ("Southern Border Program"). The program was implemented from 2014 through 2018 by President Enrique Peña Nieto. In fact, this was enacted shortly after President Barack Obama said in June 2, 2014, that the increasingly incoming migratory flows to the United States of minors travelling alone constituted an "urgent humanitarian situation" (The White House, 2014). Only five days later, President Peña Nieto was announcing the Southern Border Program, promising to take "more global responsibility in migration matters" (Gobierno de México, 2014). The program included the mobilization of military and police officers at the border, the establishment of checkpoints, roadblocks, and detention centers, but also the apprehension of immigrants without informing them of their right to seek for asylum (John et al., 2023). These programs, along with the Mérida Initiative (2007–present), are just some examples of those programs which have been directed towards reinforcing border control and ultimately reducing the passage of undocumented migrants across borders.

Over time, Mexico has also signed bilateral agreements with Guatemala, Belize, and the United States to increase border control. As explained earlier, the Merida Initiative is a bilateral agreement, in this case between Mexico and the United States to reinforce border security. In the first three years after the agreement, the United States spent $1.5 billion, a third of which went directly to increase and modernize Mexico's armed forces (Berg, 2021). In late 2021, after negotiations between the two countries, the U.S.-Mexico Bicentennial Framework for Security, Public Health, and Safe Communities wanted to revive the previous deal, again with an intent to fight criminal organizations and criminal activity taking place along and across their shared border.

Other recent mechanisms include the Migrant Protection Protocols or "Remain in Mexico Policy", approved in 2019 during Trump's administration, which allowed the Department of Homeland Security to return all irregular migrants and asylum seekers arriving through the southern border to Mexico. After the United States government announced in May 2019 that it would impose tariffs on Mexican products if Mexico did not control migration through its borders crossing into the US, an agreement was signed between the two countries. As a result, that same year, 55,000 migrants were returned to Mexico under the program (Ortega, 2023). Unfortunately, migrants detained in Mexico live in poor conditions. As the Office of the Inspector General of the United States Department of Homeland Security published in a report, they are living in detrimental conditions in the detention centers and temporary shelters where they are held in Mexico. These centers are overcrowded, poorly nourished, and in unsanitary conditions (Homeland Security, 2019b). The Inter-American Commission on Human Rights (IACHR) was concerned "regarding the impact generated by the possibility of imposing any type of commercial reprisal between two countries on the human rights of migrants, asylum seekers and refugees, whose vulnerability increases as a result" (IACHR, 2019).

When immigrants cross US-Mexico borders, they usually arrive in delicate conditions. "No Más Muertes" (No More Deaths) is a humanitarian organization based in southern Arizona dedicated to helping those migrants who have crossed the borders and are suffering in the desert, where they are walking 50 to 130 kilometers. What started as a civil initiative in 2004 has developed into a recognized organization whose activities include hiking trails and leaving water, food, socks, blankets, and other supplies, as well as first-aid treatment, among other activities. In 2018, one of its members, Scott Warren, was arrested by US agents who were staking out a humanitarian aid station in Arizona, and then faced two trials for harboring immigrants, facing a sentence that could leave him up to 20 years in prison. In 2019, after a second trial, Mr. Warren was acquitted (Armus, 2019; The Guardian, 2019; Devereaux, 2019).

Efforts to further increase control at the borders have not ceased, and the Biden administration also developed the Mexico and United States Strengthen Joint Humanitarian Plan on Migration in 2023 to "address the humanitarian situation caused by unprecedented migration flows at our shared border and in the region" to counter human smuggling and address the root causes of migration (The White House, 2023).

In January 2021, a series of legal reforms driven by civil society came into force to protect the rights of migrant children and adolescents. There were two main new additions. From the one hand, the prohibition to hold these groups in detention centers. Now children, adolescents, and their families must be placed in Social Assistance Centers of the National Family Development System of Mexico or in civil society shelters. From the other hand, the legal procedure to study their cases also changed. The National Migration Institute must refer the cases of children and adolescents to the legal offices specifically designed for these purposes and conduct a case-by-case study and take action to reunite them with family members in their countries of origin if their lives are not in danger there or refer them to an alternative protection center or program in Mexico. However, out of 98,681 minors who were detained by the National Migration Institute between January 2021 and

May 2022, only 19,067 of them (representing 29%) were processed following the guidelines of the new system (WOLE, 2023).

As stated by Meissner (2020),

> border security should be treated as a continuing management challenge and responsibility, rather than a once-and-for-all crusade to seal the border. It is unrealistic, indeed disingenuous, to contend that the measures of effective border enforcement is zero illegal crossings, as has been enshrined in U.S. law since 2006 and occupies center stage in the immigration-as-threat narrative.

Nevertheless, President López Obrador has reinforced efforts at the border, deploying over 30,000 soldiers dedicated to immigration enforcement. As a result, Mexico detained more than 307,000 migrants in 2001, the highest number ever (HRW, 2023).

Conclusion

Before 2001, the immigration system of the United States had already become more severe, some describing it as a "criminalization" of immigration law and others as a "convergence between the criminal justice and deportation systems" (Miller, 2005; Kanstroom, 2000). However, the connection between immigration and national security became much more evident after September 11, when the figure of the migrant was rapidly connected to that of a potential terrorist, and measures securitizing migration and presenting the immigrant as a security threat have not ceased ever since.

In the case of Mexico, while the country has shifted from an origin country to also being a destination one, measures to increase border control and refrain immigrants crossing into its territory have proliferated. With pressure by the US, Mexico has implemented new norms to contend migration along the southern border. And while the first law on refugees and asylum was adopted in 2011 and has been reformed twice to expand the protections of these groups, the country has not ceased to design security strategies to counter migration as an external threat from which the country needs to protect itself.

Both countries have important numbers of refugees and asylum seekers in their lands, of peoples fleeing as they fear for their lives. Yet their actions are still based on making their journeys more difficult, and in turn dangerous. And migration is profiled as a national security threat. And even those arriving to their destinations are incarcerated in detention centers, separating children from their families. The fact that the Department of Homeland Security admitted for the first time in history that white nationalism and right-wing extremism were the most significant domestic terrorist threats in the US is explanatory itself. One should wonder whether the real threat is that coming from abroad, or whether the threat comes from within.

References

AAIUSA. (2016). National security entry-exit registration system. *Arab American Institute*, Issue Brief. Retrieved November, 18, 2023, from https://d3n8a8pro7vhmx.cloudfront.net/aai/pages/9805/attachments/original/1479325332/NSEERS_ISSUE_BRIEF.pdf?1479325332

American Immigration Lawyers Association (AILA). (2023). *Bill overview: The Dignity Act of 2023 (H.R. 3599)*. Author.

Al Jazeera. (2019, November 12). *US held record 69,550 migrant children in custody in 2019: Report*. Retrieved January 4, 2024, from www.aljazeera.com/news/2019/11/12/us-held-record-69550-migrant-children-in-custody-in-2019-report

Armus, T. (2019, November 21). After helping migrants in the Arizona desert, an activist was charged with a felony. Now, he's been acquitted. *The Washington Post*. Retrieved December 4, 2023, from www.washingtonpost.com/nation/2019/11/21/arizona-activist-scott-warren-acquitted-charges-helping-migrants-cross-border/

Artola, J. (2009). Migration and security challenges on Mexico's southern border. *International Organization for Migration*. Retrieved December 1, 2023, from www.iom.int/news/migration-and-security-challenges-mexicos-southern-border

Berg, R. (2021). The bicentennial framework for security cooperation: New approach or shuffling the pillars of Mérida? *Center for Strategic and International Studies*. Retrieved December 1, 2023, from www.csis.org/analysis/bicentennial-framework-security-cooperation-new-approach-or-shuffling-pillars-merida

Bustamante, J. (2008). Report of the special rapporteur on the human rights of migrants. Mission to the United States of America. *Human Rights Council*. A/HRC/7/12/Add.2

Chebel d'Appollonia, A. (2012). *Frontiers of Fear: Immigration and Insecurity in the United States and Europe*. Ithaca, NY: Cornell University Press.

Cinoglu, H., & Altun, N. (2013). Terrorism, international migration and border control. *European Scientific Journal*, *13*(20).

Cole, D. (2002). Enemy aliens. *Stanford Law Review*, *54*(5), 953–1004.

Congress. (2019, March 27). S.894 – Domestic Terrorism Prevention Act. *Congress of the United States of America*. Retrieved January 7, 2024, from www.congress.gov/116/bills/s894/BILLS-116s894is.xml

Devereaux, R. (2019, May 4). Bodies in the borderlands. *The Intercept*. Retrieved December 4, 2023, from https://theintercept.com/2019/05/04/no-more-deaths-scott-warren-migrants-border-arizona/

Dück, E., & Lucke, R. (2019). Same old (macro-) securitization? A comparison of political reactions to major terrorist attacks in the United States and France. *Croatian International Relations Review*, (84), 6–35.

Ewing, W., Martínez, D., & Rumbaut, R. (2015). The criminalization of immigration in the United States. *American Immigration Council*, Special Report.

Frelick, B., Kysel, I., & Podkul, J. (2016). The impact of externalization of migration controls on the rights of asylum seekers and other migrants. *Journal of Migration and Human Security*, *4*(4), 190–220.

Gobierno de México. (2014). Palabras del Presidente Enrique Peña Nieto, durante la puesta en marcha del Programa Frontera Sur. *Presidencia de la República Enrique Peña Nieto*. Retrieved December 4, 2023, from www.gob.mx/epn/prensa/palabras-del-presidente-enrique-pena-nieto-durante-la-puesta-en-marcha-del-programa-frontera-sur

Herrera-Lasso, L., & Artola, J. (2011). Migración y seguridad: dilemas e interrogantes. In N. Armijo (Ed.), *Migración y seguridad: nuevo desafío en México*. México, D.F.

Homeland Security. (2019a). *Fact Sheet: DHS agreements with Guatemala, Honduras, and El Salvador*. U.S. Department of Homeland Security.

Homeland Security. (2019b). *Management alert- DHS needs to address dangerous overcrowding and prolonged detention of children and adults in the Rio Grande Valley (Redacted)*. U.S. Department of Homeland Security.

Human Rights Watch (HRW). (2023). *World report 2023: Events of 2022*. Author.

IACHR. (2019, July 23). IACHR expresses deep concern about the situation of migrants and refugees in the United States, Mexico, and Central America. *Inter-American Commission on Human Rights*, Press release. Retrieved December 4, 2023, from www.oas.org/en/iachr/media_center/PReleases/2019/180.asp

IOM. (2022). World migration report 2022. *International Organization for Migration*. Retrieved November 3, 2023, from https://publications.iom.int/books/world-migration-report-2022

Johns, M., Loschmann, C., & Arekapudi, N. (2023). *Mexico's policy response as an emerging destination for refugees, asylum-seekers, and persons in need of international protection. Background paper to the 'World Development Report 2023: Migrants, Refugees, and Societies*. United Nations High Commissioner for Refugees

Kanstroom, D. (2000). Deportation, social control and punishment: Some thoughts about why hard laws make bad cases. *Harvard Law Review*, *113*(8), 1890–1935.

Kerwin, D. (2005). The use and misuse of 'National Security' rationale in crafting U.S. refugee and immigration policies. *International Journal of Refugee Law*, *17*, 749–763.

Meissner, D. (2020). Rethinking the U.S.-Mexico border immigration enforcement system. *Migration Policy Institute*. Retrieved December, 4, 2023, from www.migrationpolicy.org/sites/default/files/publications/rethinking-enforcement-roadmap_final.pdf

Migration Policy Institute. (2001). Background paper: Immigration and national security. *Migration Policy Institute*. Retrieved November, 18, 2023, from www.migrationpolicy.org/research/background-paper-immigration-and-national-security

Miller, T. (2005). Blurring the boundaries between immigration and crime control after September 11th. *Boston College Third World Law Journal*, *25*(1), 87.

Ortega, E. (2023). Containing unwanted migration: Securitization discourses used by the United States to outsource its border to Mexico from 1988 to 2020. *Inter Disciplina*, *11*(29).

Parker, A., & Patten, W. (2004). Letter to U.S. Senate and House of Representatives regarding the "Clear Law Enforcement for Criminal Alien Removal Act of 2003. *Human Rights Watch*. Retrieved November, 22, 2023, from www.hrw.org/news/2004/04/20/letter-us-senate-and-house-representatives-regarding-clear-law-enforcement-criminal

Ramos-García, J. M., Barrachina-Lisón, C., and Ramos, J. E. (2020). The southern border of Mexico: Problems and challenges of national security and its different dimensions. *Política, Globalidad y Ciudadanía*, 6(12), 102–127. Retrieved December 4, 2023, from www.redalyc.org/journal/6558/655868422006/html/#redalyc_655868422006_ref68

Ribando, C., & Finklea, K. (2017). *US-Mexican security cooperation: The Mérida Initiative and beyond* (Report). US Congressional Research Service.

Taylor, M. (2002). Immigration enforcement post-September 11: Safeguarding the civil rights of Middle Eastern-American and immigrant communities. *Georgetown Immigration Law Journal*, *17*(1), 63–114.

The Guardian. (2019). Arizona activist who gave migrants humanitarian aid acquitted in second trial. Retrieved December 3, 2023, from www.theguardian.com/us-news/2019/nov/20/arizona-activist-migrants-trial-scott-warren

The White House. (2002). Border security: U.S. – Mexico border partnership agreement. *The White House*. Retrieved December 4, 2023, from https://georgewbush-whitehouse.archives.gov/infocus/usmxborder/

The White House. (2014, June 2). Presidential memorandum – response to the influx of unaccompanied alien children across the southwest border. *The White House*. Retrieved December 4, 2023, from https://obamawhitehouse.archives.gov/the-press-office/2014/06/02/presidential-memorandum-response-influx-unaccompanied-alien-children-acr

The White House. (2021, January 20). Fact Sheet: President Biden sends immigration bill to congress as part of his commitment to modernize our immigration system. *The White House*. Retrieved November 15, 2023, from www.whitehouse.gov/briefing-room/statements-releases/2021/01/20/fact-sheet-president-biden-sends-immigration-bill-to-congress-as-part-of-his-commitment-to-modernize-our-immigration-system/

The White House. (2023, May 2). Mexico and United States strengthen joint humanitarian plan on migration. *The White House*. Retrieved December 1, 2023, from www.whitehouse.gov/briefing-room/statements-releases/2023/05/02/mexico-and-united-states-strengthen-joint-humanitarian-plan-on-migration/

UN DESA. (2020). International migrant stock 2020. *United Nations Department of Economic and Social Affairs, Population Division*. Retrieved December 1, 2023, from www.un.org/development/desa/pd/content/international-migrant-stock

UNHCR. (2023). Refugee data finder. *United Nations High Commissioner for Refugees*. Retrieved December 1, 2023, from www.unhcr.org/refugee-statistics/

Vandenberg, Q. (2004). How can the United States rectify its post-9/11 stance on noncitizens' rights. *Notre Dame Journal of Law, Ethics & Public Policy*, *18*(2), 605–646.

Walia, H. (2021). *Border and rule: Global migration, capitalism and the rise of racist nationalism*. Haymarket Books.

Waslin, M. (2009). Immigration policy and the Latino community since 9/11. In T. Givens, G. Freeman, & D. Leal (Eds.), *Immigration policy and security. U.S., Europe, and commonwealth perspectives*. Routledge.

WOLE. (2023). Migrant children and adolescents are at risk as Mexico and the United States fail to provide protections. *Washington Office on Latin America*. Retrieved December 5, 2023, from www.wola.org/analysis/migrant-children-adolescents-risk-mexico-united-states-fail-protections/

6

Securitizing migration in the European Union

Overview of securitization practices in the European Union

Studying the case of the European Union is particularly interesting for two reasons. From the one hand, it is because this is not a case study of individual states, as the other chapters have done. On the other hand, its analysis is thought-provoking precisely because of its characteristics and because the EU has been a symbol of the advancement of liberalism and democracy. While this chapter will focus mostly on the security framework that has advanced in the EU context in the field of migration and security, there are numerous examples showing how its Member States have individually advanced towards the securitization of migration.[1] At the same time, the study of the EU in the context of a liberal actor can be used to expose this actor as one breaching the values it has so often acclaimed. This chapter will thus offer an overview of securitization practices to reach the conclusion that even those actors wishing to become liberal models are also ones dealing with migration as security threats.

Two of the most dangerous and overflowing migratory routes in the world are in Europe. One is the Eastern Mediterranean Route, and the other is the Mediterranean Sea Route. The first of these passages is used by those migrants trying to reach the European Union through Turkey, making their way to Greece, Cyprus, and Bulgaria. Since the outbreak of the Syrian war in 2011, this route has become more crowded. But after rising numbers in 2015,

1 By way of illustration, Bourbeau studies securitization practices of France and Canada in Bourbeau, P. (2011). *The securitization of migration. A study of movement and order*. Routledge; Karyotis uncovers the case of Greece in Karyotis, G. (2012). Securitization of migration in Greece: Process, motives, and implications. *International Political Sociology*, *5*(4), 390–408; Bello does so in the case of Italy in Bello, V. (2021). The spiral of prejudice and the securitization of migration. *International Political Science*, *16*(2), 58–73; or Palander and Pellander in the case of Finland in Palander, J., & Pellander, S. (2019). Mobility and the security paradigm: How immigration became securitized in Finnish law and policy. *Journal of FinnishSstudies*, *22*(1&2), 173–193.

DOI: 10.4324/9781003458159-8

the European Union signed an agreement with Turkey in March 2016 to contend migratory flows and reduce the number of irregular arrivals through the later country. Between January and September 2023, 2,500 people had already lost their lives in this Mediterranean Sea Route, while trying to cross the Mediterranean to reach the European Union. During the same period, another 186,000 had successfully reached Europe, about 83% of whom arrived in Italy (Security Council, 2023). According to IOM (2023), the first quarter of 2023 was the deadliest first quarter since 2017. The organization has also registered over 20,000 migrant deaths recorded in this route between 2014 and 2023.

These extensive numbers of incoming migrants led to a collapse of national reception systems, and states felt like they had lost control over migration and their frontiers. If a new securitization wave had already started in Europe after the events of 9/11, the increasing numbers of migratory fluxes in 2015–2016 led to the reinforcement of securitization measures to refrain unwanted migration from reaching EU territories. Again, migration was presented as a threat to national security, and discourses on the need to protect from this 'external threat' grew once again.

This was not the first time in the history of the EU to connect migration to security. In fact, the adoption of the 1990 Schengen Agreements – which became consolidated with the approval of the 1992 Maastricht Treaty and the 1997 Treaty of Amsterdam – already drew a connection between immigration and crime (Chebel d'Appollonia, 2017). With the approval of these instruments, the distinction between internal and external security became blurred and instead of focusing on border management to control immigration, Member States started focusing on "threat management" (Huysmans, 1995; Bigo & Guild, 2005; Chebel d'Appollonia, 2017). A trend to liberalize migration at the EU level, as many had hoped as the millennium began, shifted towards the opposite direction after the events of 9/11. For the first time in its history, NATO invoked its Article 5 self-defense clause (Chebel d'Appollonia, 2012). Immediately after 9/11, the European Union designed a response to these terrorist attacks. The Justice and Home Affairs Council met that same month and designed a package of measures. The European Council held an extraordinary meeting to endorse it and launched an "Action Plan to Combat Terrorism" which provided a collective response (European Council, 2001).

Resources directed to EU immigration policy have since then been spent towards terrorism and police matters (Luedtke, 2009). Member States have all applied their own measures to stop and control migration flows, but there has also been cooperation at the EU level. The EU has passed a series of policy measures to control incoming immigrants; from lengthening the requirements to obtain visas, to increasing border control and detaining and deporting those who overstay or who enter irregularly. But it was not until the Tampere Conclusions that the European Council decided that a Common

European Asylum System should be implemented. Thus, the EU started designing a common EU asylum and migration policy to address political and human rights issues, enhancing greater coherence for the national and international policies of Member States. This process was further enhanced in 2004, when the Hague Programme implemented minimum standards for a common asylum procedure. It finally culminated with the Treaty of Lisbon, which transformed these measures from minimum standards to creating a single asylum procedure. Since the application of the latter agreement, Article 80 of the Treaty on the Functioning of the European Union (TFEU) also incorporated the principle of solidarity and fair sharing of responsibility between Member States in these matters (European Parliament, 2018). Over time, measures to control immigration at the EU level have advanced, also following an exterior dimension approach (Olesti, 2010).

Since Dublin III entered into force in July 2013, the procedures to protect asylum applicants and to improve the efficiency of the system were reinforced.[2] However, the large-scale and so-called refugee crisis questioned the effectiveness of the Dublin System, and a revision was conducted in 2016, leading to the proposal of Dublin IV Regulation. This would enhance the capacity of the system to determine a particular Member State responsible for examining an application and ensure a fair sharing of this responsibility between them, based on a solidarity principle.

In the past years, many Directives and Regulations on migration have been enacted. The Eurodac Regulation establishes a fingerprint database by which the EU can identify all asylum seekers (European Dactyloscopy). This system, established in 2003, was the first multinational biometric system in the world. Eurodac now also serves the implementation of Regulation No. 604/20133 (the commonly known 'Dublin Regulation') and altogether these seek to assist in deciding which is the Member State responsible for an asylum application.

Another measure which has been quite discussed is the Returns Directive (2008/115/EC). This sets out common standards for returning irregular migrants from third countries. The Directive 2008/115/EC on common standards and procedures in Member States for returning illegally staying third-country nationals (hereafter Return Directive) was approved in June 2008 by the European Parliament. The main purpose of the Directive is to lay down a set of rules and procedures for all Member States on the return of illegal immigrants within the Union. Although every state can still decide whether

2 In 2013, a group of legislative documents was passed to strengthen and further establish the proceedings, rights, and obligations of Member States and asylum seekers and following the Common European Asylum System. The Reception Conditions Directive (Directive 2013/33/EU) also sets minimum standards for the reception of asylum seekers in the EU, and the Asylum Procedures Directives (Directive 2013/32/EU) sets minimum standards on procedures for granting and withdrawing the status of refugee.

it wishes to regularize or deport an immigrant in its territory, the goal of the norm is to apply it once this decision has been taken. It then sets periods of custody, re-entry bans, and other similar regularizations. For the first time at the EU level, the Directive established mandatory return decisions, the preference for voluntary return, the mandatory issuance of entry bans along with return decisions, procedural safeguards in these processes, and grounds for pre-removal detention (European Parliament, 2020).

On September 12, 2018, the commission published a recast proposal of the Return Directive[3] arguing that it needed to "notably reduce the length of return procedures, secure a better link between asylum and return procedures and ensure a more effective use of measures to prevent absconding".[4] The new Return Directive is thence another step towards expelling certain groups of migrants more easily throughout the Union. In addition, Europol became an important actor in the counter-terrorist strategy of the European Union, and its role was reinforced after 9/11 with the introduction of new activities. In 2016, it was also reinforced with the creation of the European Counter Terrorism Centre (ECTC) as a specialized hub focused on designing operations and providing a comprehensive response to contend the terrorist threat.

Furthermore, a clear symptom of securitization in the EU is the way in which this has coordinated and developed coastal border control. The European Coastguard is an entity created "to integrate national border security systems of Member States against all kinds of threats that could happen at or through the external border of Member States" (Abbott, 2013). Boat migration has been considered as a threat requiring of a border security response, and the EU has increased the militarization response of migrant watercrafts. And EU practice in these matters "presents compelling examples of securitizing search and rescue in the context of boat migration, which has distorted the primary humanitarian object of the regime" (Ghezelbash et al., 2018). Frontex has continuously increased in size and scope, which in turn has also meant a reinforcement of its militarized border force. In 2020, a report published by a group of media outlets claimed that Frontex was involved in pushback practices in the Aegean Sea to force out migrant boats from EU waters (Fallon, 2020). As explained by Moreno-Lax:

> While legal amendments have accompanied a change in official language, giving rise to an account where "saving lives" features as top

3 Proposal for a Directive of the European Parliament and of the Council on common standards and procedures in Member States for returning illegally staying third-country nationals (recast) A contribution from the European Commission to the Leaders' meeting in Salzburg on 19–20 September 2018 COM/2018/634 final. https://eur-lex.europa.eu/legal-content/EN/TXT/?uri=COM:2018:0634:FIN

4 European Commission, COM(2018) 634, explanatory memorandum, 12 September 2018, p. 2.

> priority, this has not resulted in an equal transformation of practices on the ground. Neither policy goals, nor their underpinning rationale or the means to achieve them have been revised. The reduction of unauthorized arrivals remains the constant goal, and interdiction the constant tool to attain it.
>
> (Moreno-Lax, 2018)

These securitization measures have also been captured in various Agendas on Migration. In view of the migrant and refugee crisis since 2014, the Commission issued the European Agenda on Migration, which introduced the hotspots to register and control incoming migrants, controlled between the European Border and Coast Guard Agency (EASO, formerly Frontex) and Europol. A set of systems has since then been implemented not only to manage the arrival of migrants and asylum applications, but also to reinforce security at the border. In this sense, the Schengen Information System helps provide information on, for instance, wanted or missing persons and entry bans in a database which is accessible to all police offers and law enforcement officials of the EU. The Visa Information System, on the other hand, refers to a common visa policy and cooperation between Member States, controlling the issuing of visas and its control by officials at border points (European Parliament, 2018).

The New Strategic Agenda for the period 2019–2024 differs from the previous one in the approach used to deal with migration. While both strategies seek to fight against illegal migration, in the first one the idea was to reinforce skilled labor from third countries, while in 2019, the EU considered the protection of external borders as an absolute prerequisite for the security of Europeans. The asylum and returns policy along with border enforcement are much more reinforced in the latest agenda, although the issue of how to establish a harmonized and comprehensive European policy to address immigration is rather vague.

More recently, the New Pact on Migration and Asylum (hereafter "New Pact") has taken the stage. This was one of the flagship proposals of President Ursula von der Leyen in 2020 and after three years of negotiations, the Council and the European Parliament finally agreed on its final content in December 2023. The instrument consists of a legal framework that establishes consistent rules for all Member States on migration. As in the past years countries have taken unilateral and uncoordinated steps to deal with the arrival of asylum seekers; the New Pact seeks to balance the principles of responsibility and solidarity among the Union, including a system of mandatory solidarity to distribute migratory pressure more evenly through a "solidarity pool". The agreement covers five main regulations: (a) the Screening Regulation, (b) the Eurodac Regulation, (c) the Asylum Procedures Regulation, (d) the Asylum Migration Management Regulation, and (e) the Crisis and Force Majeure Regulation.

The Screening Regulation designs a pre-entry procedure to offer a rapid examination of the asylum seeker who arrived at the EU, which is then stored in the European Dactyloscopy (Eurodac) database system. While the Asylum Procedures Regulation accelerates all return and border procedures, on the other hand, the Crisis and Force Majeure Regulation consists of a set of rules that will apply in times of sudden and massive arrival of asylum seekers and refugees, thinking of resolving situations such as the 2015 migratory crisis or the Covid-19 pandemic. In these cases, Member States will be allowed to apply harder security measures such as extending the border procedure and detention times for up to 20 weeks.

Countries like Germany and NGOs have voiced concerns, arguing that this regulation could infringe the principle of non-refoulement and degrade the rights of children (Liboreiro & Genovese, 2023). The International Rescue Committee has called the Pact a "migration policy risk exacerbating rather than solving existing challenges such as decreasing pressure on states of first entry, limiting violence at the borders, and creating a Common European Asylum System with clear rules and regulations" (IRC, 2023). The organization is concerned that the instrument will allow ineffective monitoring mechanisms, the facilitation of pushbacks, and an overall violation of migrants' rights without any oversight or accountability. Amnesty International also finds the Pact problematic and has declared that it sets "European asylum law back for decades to come" as it is "designed to make it harder for people to access safety" (Amnesty International, 2023). In sum, the main concerns are regarding the reduction of safeguards for people seeking asylum in the EU, such as the reinforcement of border asylum procedures, the facilitation of detention at EU borders, the harshening of access to asylum and legal support at the border, and the externalization of migration management as it builds on recent deals with third countries. This shows a prevalence for maintaining the security of EU states over that of refugees. On a similar direction are the comments by Stępka (2023):

> The New Pact on Migration and Asylum as a securitizing move is strongly embedded within the migration-security continuum and existing security logics. It follows risk management and resilience, underlining the need to maintain control over the EU border and increased migratory movements. . . . In this vein, the pact moves the migration-security continuum slightly towards "exceptionalism", while still strongly investing in practices and technologies of risk management and resilience.
>
> (Stępka, 2023)

In addition to this, there is also an external dimension that is operationalized by EU readmission agreements with non-Member States. In this sense, the EU has also sought to reinforce cooperation with third countries such as Turkey, Libya, and Tunisia, as also shown by the application of the Global Approach to Migration and Mobility, a tool to design a framework of external migration and asylum policy. A very controversial agreement with a non-Member State was that signed with Turkey. In this case, illegal migrants and asylum seekers who arrive to EU land from Turkey are returned to the latter country in exchange for visa liberalization for Turkish citizens and a payment of 6 billion euros under the Facility for Refugees in Turkey (European Parliament, 2018).

Other agreements to externalize border and migration control include Ukraine. Before the armed conflict with Russia began, this was an important transit country for migrants coming from other regions, and Kiev increased border control efforts to retain asylum seekers trying to reach EU land. In July 2023, the European Commission also signed a controversial pact with Tunisia to fight irregular migration (European Commission, 2023). In this case, 127 million euros are made available in budget support to the latter country as a response to an increase in boats leaving North Africa and making their way to Europe (Al Jazeera, 2023; Reuters, 2023).

These practices lead to further securitization of migration in the EU. And along with the 'crisification' of external borders, these have become a system of governance in its own right (Moreno-Lax, 2023). As such, externalization measures have raised concerns on the avoidance of judicial and democratic accountability (Molinari, 2019; European Parliament, 2020). Webber (2017) has pointed out that the deals signed with African countries prevent "citizens leaving some of the most repressive and conflict-ridden states in Africa" and in turn mean that the EU is not willing to protect the rights of these migrants and instead prioritizes refraining them from leaving the continent. As Oxfam International (2016) also denounced, "by choosing to outsource to third countries Europe's border control and the responsibility for managing migration, Europe attempts to outsource its obligations to respect human rights".

Conclusion

The EU has presented immigration as a security threat on many occasions. And although passing certain instruments claiming the rights of migrants, including refugees and asylum seekers, their rights are nevertheless undermined by the approval of policy initiatives based on an idea to refrain them from reaching the Union and persistently framing them as a security threat. Over time, these groups have been associated with the fight against organized crime, human trafficking, terrorism, and drugs control (Furuseth, 2003).

As explained in PICUM's report, "the current emphasis on border control in Europe significantly overshadows the need to address other causes of irregularity, such as inadequate visa and residence policies, administrative failures and difficulties in understanding the complex procedures of residence and work permits" (Manieri & LeVoy, 2015). Furthermore, the lack of any impact assessment makes it impossible to determine whether, for instance, the Return Directive has affected return rates or if there is a need for additional EU action. Still, the need to ensure the protection of human rights of third-country nationals in the EU while ensuring fair and effective return procedures persists.

Since the events of September 11, but also more forcefully since the migratory crisis, what we have seen is an increase in normative and policy measures to deal with migration through the lens of security. The Agendas on Migration, the European Security Agenda, investment in increasing border control, the expansion of externalization agreements, and the enlargement of Frontex forces are just but a few of the examples showing that the strategy of the Union is based on dealing with migration as a security threat, instead of one based on human security.

Conflicts in the world are increasing, and the climate crisis will bring more drought, floods, and devastation. As a result, the numbers of refugees and asylum seekers will likely continue to grow in the coming years. As the security strategies of the European Union foresee, migration will continue to be a top priority issue. However, it is in the hands of the EU to decide whether it let itself fall into the hands of a new order based on the preference for national security and geopolitical concerns, or whether it wants to continue representing the liberal democratic values it has upheld for so long.

References

Abbott, T. (2013, August 25). Address to the 2013 Federal coalition campaign launch. *Brisbane.*

Al Jazeera. (2023, September 22). EU to start releasing money to Tunisia under migration pact. *Al Jazeera.* Retrieved November, 15, 2023, from www.aljazeera.com/news/2023/9/22/eu-to-start-releasing-money-to-tunisia-under-migration-pact

Amnesty International. (2023, December 20). EU: Migration Pact agreement will lead to a "surge in suffering". Retrieved January 2, 2024, from www.amnesty.org/en/latest/news/2023/12/eu-migration-pact-agreement-will-lead-to-a-surge-in-suffering/

Bigo, D., & Guild, E. (2005). *Controlling frontiers: Free movement into and within Europe.* Routledge.

Burch Elias, S., Kevin Cope, K., & Goldenziel, J. (Eds.). (forthcoming). *The Oxford handbook of comparative immigration law.* Oxford University Press.

Chebel d'Appollonia, A. (2012). *Frontiers of fear: Immigration and insecurity in the United States and Europe.* Cornell University Press.

Chebel d'Appollonia, A. (2017). Xenophobia, racism and the securitization of immigration. In P. Bourbeau (Ed.), *Handbook on migration and security.* Edwar Elgar Publishing Limited.

European Commission. (2023, September 22). Commission announces almost €127 million in support of the implementation of the Memorandum of Understanding with Tunisia and in line with the 10-point plan for Lampedusa. *Directorate-General for Neighbourhood and Enlargement Negotiations of the European Commission.* Retrieved November, 15, 2023, from https://neighbourhood-enlargement.ec.europa.eu/news/commission-announces-almost-eu127-million-support-implementation-memorandum-understanding-tunisia-2023-09-22_en

European Council. (2001). Conclusions and plan of action of the extraordinary European Council meeting on 21 September 2001. SN 140/01.
European Parliament. (2018). Migration and Asylum: A challenge for Europe, European Parliament. Fact Sheets on the European Union, PE 600.414.
European Parliament. (2020). The return directive 2008/115/EC: European implementation assessment. European Parliamentary Research Service, PE 642.840.
Fallon, K. (2020). EU border force 'complicit' in illegal campaign to stop refugees landing. *The Guardian*, October 24. Retrieved November, 29, 2023, from www.theguardian.com/global-development/2020/oct/24/eu-border-force-complicit-in-campaign-to-stop-refugees-landing
Furuseth, R. (2003). *Creating security through immigration control: An analysis of European immigration discourse and the development towards a common EU asylum and immigration policy*. Norwegian Institute of International Affairs.
Ghezelbash, D., Moreno-Lax, V., Klein, N., & Opeskin, B. (2018). Securitization of search and rescue at sea: The response to boat migration in the Mediterranean and offshore Australia. *International and Comparative Law Quarterly*, *67*(2), 315–351.
Huysmans, J. (1995). Migrants as a security problem: Dangers of 'securitizing' societal issues. In R. Miles & D. Thrähardt (Eds.), *Migration and European integration: The dynamics of inclusion and exclusion*. Pinter Publishers.
IOM. (2023). Deadliest quarter for migrants in the Central Mediterranean since 2017. *International Organization for Migration*. Retrieved November 8, 2023, from www.iom.int/news/deadliest-quarter-migrants-central-mediterranean-2017
IRC. (2023, October 27). What is the EU Pact on migration and asylum? *International Rescue Committee*. Retrieved January 2, 2024, from www.rescue.org/eu/article/what-eu-pact-migration-and-asylum
Liboreiro, J., & Genovese, V. (2023, October 4). In new breakthrough, EU countries agree new rules to manage future migration crises. *Euronews*. Retrieved November, 15, 2023, from www.euronews.com/my-europe/2023/10/04/eu-countries-agree-new-rules-to-deal-with-future-migration-crises-after-italy-compromises
Luedtke, A. (2009). Fortifying Fortress Europe? The effect of September 11 on EU immigration policy. In T. Givens, G. Freeman, & D. Leal (Eds.), *Immigration policy and security. U.S., Europe, and commonwealth perspectives*. Routledge.
Manieri, M., & LeVoy, M. (2015). PICUM position paper on EU return directive. *Platform for International Cooperation on Undocumented Migrants*. Retrieved November, 17, 2023, from www.statewatch.org/media/documents/news/2015/apr/eu-picum-report-on-returns-policy.pdf
Maurice, E., & Menneteau, M. (2019). *From crisis exit to world challenges: The EU's Strategic Agenda 2019* (European Issues, No. 521). Foundation Robert Schuman.
Molinari, C. (2019). The EU and its perilous journey through the migration crisis: Informalisation of the EU return policy and rule of law concerns. *European Law Review*, *44*(6), 824–840.
Moreno-Lax, V. (2018). The EU humanitarian border and the securitization of human rights: The 'rescue-through-interdiction/rescue-without-protection' paradigm. *Journal of Common Market Studies*, *56*(1), 119–140.
Moreno-Lax, V. (2023). The "crisification" of migration law: Insights from the EU external border. *Queen Mary Law Research Paper No. 403/2023*.
Olesti, A. (2010). La normative y las políticas de la Unión Europea en 2008. In E. Aja, J. Arango, & J. Oliver (Eds.), *La inmigración en tiempos de crisis. Anuario de la inmigración en España*. Edicions Bellaterra.

Oxfam International. (2016, June 7). *Migration compact is attempt to outsource Eu's obligation to respect human rights.* Retrieved November 15, 2023, from www.oxfam.org/es/node/9025

Reuters. (2023, September 22). EU to disburse $135 mln to Tunisia as part of migration pact. *Reuters.* Retrieved November, 15, 2023, from www.reuters.com/world/africa/eu-disburse-135-mln-tunisia-part-migration-pact-2023-09-22/

Security Council. (2023). Conflicts, disasters driving more migrants to risk mediterranean crossing briefers warn security council ahead of Libya mandate decision. Security Council, 9428th Meeting, SC/15427, Meetings Coverage and Press Releases. Retrieved November 8, 2023, from https://press.un.org/en/2023/sc15427.doc.htm

Stępka, M. (2023). The new pact on migration and asylum: Another step in the EU migration-security continuum or preservation of the status quo? *Bialystok Legal Studies*, *28*(1).

Webber, F. (2017). Europe's unknown war. *Race & Class*, *59*(1), 36–53.

7

Securitizing migration in Asia and Oceania

Migration in the Asian region: the cases of Malaysia and Indonesia

The Southeast Asian region is of particular interest to study through the lens of international migration. While North America and Europe remain important destination regions, most of the migrants in Southeast Asia are moving within the continent. Labor migration is an important reason why many decide to leave, which in turn makes dependence on remittances quite significant. But as conflicts spread and intensify in Asia, the number of displaced persons also increases significantly.

Asia and the Pacific region were hosting 6.8 million refugees, 5 million internally displaced people and 1.2 million stateless persons by the end of 2022 (UNHCR, 2022). In the past years, different conflicts have resulted in massive migratory movements from different countries. The conflict in Afghanistan following the Taliban's takeover in 2021 became a humanitarian crisis with millions of Afghans fleeing to Iran and Pakistan. The coup d'état of the Myanmar military against the civilian government of early 2021 installed a state of emergency and destroyed hopes of democratic progress in the country. This political crisis has also created more than 1.1 million refugees and asylum seekers (UNHCR, 2023a).

Many of those using the Southeast Asian Route are Muslim Rohingya refugees fleeing political repression in Myanmar. Violence against this minority began in the Rakhine State in the late 1970s with military Operation Dragon King, but other operations and violence against them have remained since. One of the biggest exoduses took place in 2017, when Myanmar forced more than 700,000 people to cross the border into Bangladesh in a military crackdown (UN News, 2023; Bhattacharyya, 2023). These migrants were then moving to Indonesia, Malaysia, and Thailand.

In fact, these three countries – Malaysia, Thailand, and Indonesia – are the ones hosting more than 99% of refugees and asylum seekers in Southeast Asia (UN DESA, 2020). Among the three, Indonesia and Malaysia are classified as being the most democratic (EIU, 2023) and "freer" (Freedom House, 2023a, 2023b). This is not to say that they both don't have significant democratic

DOI: 10.4324/9781003458159-9

deficiencies, but they are higher ranked, according to these studies, than Thailand. This has been an important factor to consider when deciding to analyze them. Additionally, Malaysia and Indonesia are both origin, transit, and destination countries. This makes them particularly interesting for the purposes of this study. Also, there are significant concerns regarding the treatment of migrants in these countries. Thence studying them can be a good basis to see securitization practices in the field of migration in the Asian region.

In early 2021, there were already 13,700 refugees and asylum seekers in Indonesia coming from 40 different countries, although more than half of these were refugees from Afghanistan (MMC, 2021). In 2020, two thirds of those arriving to Indonesia were Rohingya, but many use it only as a transit country to reach Malaysia (MMC, 2021). In the period between January 2022 and August 2023, about 1,400 Rohingya refugees were known to have arrived by sea in Indonesia, and another 500 in Malaysia (UNHCR, 2023b). Another important destination country for those travelling through Indonesia is Australia. As a result, bilateral relations have been strengthened in the past years with the aim to build stronger border controls and refrain migrants reaching Oceania. In sum, as these countries become important transit and destination countries for migrants in general and refugees in particular, it is interesting to study the extent to which their rights are protected, or to what extent they have been limited in the name of sovereignty and national security.

Therefore, there are many reasons to see the cases of Malaysia and Indonesia as being particularly interesting for analysis. From the one hand, as explained, these countries deal with an important number of migratory movements within the region. From the other, because they are not signatories of the 1951 Convention Relating to the Status of Refugees nor of its 1967 Protocol, refugees in these countries already have less rights guaranteed than in those countries' parties of the 1951 Convention. The emphasis on being part of this international instrument is relevant because since refugees are vulnerable groups, if the state is not a signatory of a basic instrument to protect their rights, it is likely that the protection of their human rights is worsened. Nevertheless, it is still interesting to study these countries in comparison to others since they are also active agents securitizing migration. And thus it is crucial to understand the measures and contexts on which the securitization is designed. A party may be a signatory of international instruments protecting human rights or not, and it can have one political regime type or another, but they are all interesting to scrutinize to compare their levels and methods in the securitization of migration process.

The case of Malaysia

Malaysia is the 17th country receiving more international migration in the world since the 1960s (MPI, 2020). While in 2022 there were 2.2 million documented migrant workers in the country, unofficial estimates range from 1.2 to 3.5 million, thus making Malaysia one of the largest receiving countries in the Southeast Asian region (IOM, 2023). According to UNHCR, there are about 185,000 refugees and asylum seekers registered with the agency, including 100,000 ethnic Rohingya Muslims (HRW, 2023).

Even though the economy in the country is strongly dependent on foreign labor in sectors such as construction, manufacturing, and agriculture, the Malaysian government has been applying harsh security measures since the 1990s, when massive crackdowns and the arrest of illegal migrants began. The industries in the country need low-skilled workers and there is high demand for low-wage labor. Yet as immigrants contribute to the economy of the country, and are in fact essential to its economic growth, they are still constructed as security threats. Undocumented migrants have often been treated as a "public enemy" by Malaysian authorities and as a threat to national security (Kudo, 2013).

Policies such as the Ops Nyah I and II (meaning "Operation Get Rid"), first applied in 1991, targeted illegal migrants, and led to thousands of arrests. Later, Prime Minister Mahathir approved an additional measure to reduce dependency on Indonesian workers which consisted in replacing them with migrants from other countries. The idea was to "Hire Indonesians last", arguing that because of the "crime they have committed, we've kept silent about. But when a riot is carried out by one group, followed by another and another, we cannot any longer stay silent" (Liow, 2006). Furthermore, in 2002, the Immigration Act of 1959 was amended to include a provision that would lead to imprisonment for up to five years for those migrants who violated immigration law (SUARAM, 2002). Migrants, including refugees, have long been seen as social threats. They have been referred to as those committing crimes, spreading diseases, and supporting politically subversive activities, a discourse that has been enhanced since the events of 9/11.

The Immigration Act No. 1154 was passed in 2002 with the goal to search and fine or imprison illegal migrants residing in the country. Thus, any irregular migrant, including refugees and asylum seekers, automatically became a threat to the country and its sovereignty (Mahalingam, 2022). Furthermore, a set of Special Immigration Courts was established just a few years later in different immigration detention centers to speed up the process of resolving the cases of so many detainees. Today, there are almost 90% of them coming from Myanmar, with 58% being Rohingya (IOM, 2023). We need not forget that Malaysia is not a signatory of the 1951 Convention Relating to the Status of Refugees nor to its 1967 Protocol, thus refugees and asylum seekers face different circumstances in the country since they are less safeguarded. Consequences are, for instance, that a person with the profile of a refugee is instead categorized as an illegal immigrant upon arrival to the country.

Furthermore, there is currently no legislative or administrative framework for dealing with refugees. This situation is similar to its neighboring Thailand, as the latter has no special laws focusing on refugees either. Therefore, all refugees entering both Malaysia and Thailand without a visa are automatically considered illegal immigrants. Notwithstanding, the Malaysian government has worked with the UNHCR Malaysia office to register refugees under the procedural standards of Refugee Status Determination. However, the government has denied the agency access to immigration detention centers since mid-2019, which has made difficult the protection of those immigrants in detention by the UN agency since then (HRW, 2023). In addition, in September 2022, the national security council director-general proposed shutting down UNHCR's presence in the country so that the government could manage refugees and asylum seekers without "foreign interference" (Vinothaa, 2022; FMT, 2022). Over time, the government has continuously presented migrants and refugees as societal threats who commit crimes and spread diseases. And in addition to increasing border controls, the government has also reinforced immigration raids, leading to the detention of immigrants and the following repatriation of many in the country. An important feature of these practices is that they have progressively been carried out by civilian volunteers reinforced by national authorities.

Another example of how migrants are treated as threats is the creation of the People's Volunteer Corps (*Jabatan Sukarelawan Malaysia*), commonly known as Rela, a paramilitary civil volunteer corps created by the government to control undocumented migration in the country. Following the Essential Amendment Regulations 2005 and Operation Disciplined ("Ops Tegas"), the group is fully allowed to conduct interrogations and demand all documents which they consider necessary. They are also allowed to enter and search both public and private premises without a search warrant to bear firearms. This increased power of the Rela forces also allows the detention of "undesirable persons" or those suspected of being in an irregular condition.

Since the group was created, it has raided communities of Rohingya refugees and other immigrant communities without supervision or permission from immigrant authorities. Following these raids where they use excessive force, destroy property and identity documents, many of these refugees and asylum seekers are then sent to immigration detention camps. In these camps, the chances of being repatriated and therefore of also violating the principle of non-refoulement increase and become rather common (Amnesty International, 2007). With the Approval of the Malaysia Volunteers Corps Act 2012, some restrictions were introduced, such as the prohibition to carry firearms and make arrests. However, criticism against these bodies for the treatment given to migrants has persisted, and so are the accusations that Rela is a machinery to maintain the security of the present political regime (Kudo, 2013). In February 2021, the government deported 1,086 individuals to Myanmar, despite this country having undergone a military coup just a few weeks earlier (Amnesty International, 2023).

Contributing to this negative perception of migration, speech acts by government authorities have long treated immigrants as a threat and have openly shown their rejection to refugees. In 2015, after 2,000 Rohingya were rescued from people-smuggling boats, Malaysia's deputy home minister, Wan Junaidi Tuanku Jaafar, said publicly that "We don't want them to come here. . . . I would like them to be turned back and ask them to go back to their own country. We cannot tell them we are welcoming them" (The Guardian, 2015).

Ethnicity also plays a key role for the reception of migrants. Those coming from countries of a Muslim identity are given considerably better treatment than those who are not from Muslim ethnicity. The first have access to education, employment, and other services, while the latter do not (Isa, 2017). Politicians have also used ethnicity to place a threat to those who do not have Muslim identity, claiming that migrants wanted to inseminate Christianity amongst Malays. It is not only politicians who have added to this securitization, as the media have also propagated the use of terms like 'Indons', 'illegals', and 'troublemakers' to refer derogatorily to Indonesian migrants. They have been portrayed as a criminal threat, as increasing the crime rates, and have been presumed to be criminals (May, 2015). In 2017, the Malaysian government also initiated a tracking system for refugees to identify them and know their whereabouts. This "Tracking Refugees Information System" (TRIS) has become yet another mechanism to deal with migration as a national security issue. The same website of the government states that refugee control is critical for the safety of the country, as they can be the source to produce social problems.

Border externalization has become a rather common practice in the country, as authorities are blocking the arrival of boats by sea. In 2020, Defense Minister Ismail Sabri stated that Malaysian authorities had turned away 22 boats with Rohingya refugees between January and May of the same year. Many of these boats are in life-threatening conditions, yet the government of Malaysia refuses to help them and makes them return to where they came from, failing with international obligations to search and rescue (HRW, 2021).

Migration between Indonesia and Malaysia is also common, with Indonesian nationals going to Malaysia looking for better economic prospects. There are an estimated 2.7 million Indonesian workers in Malaysia (Llewellyn, 2021b). While Indonesian immigration going to Malaysia was rather common and welcome in Malaysia during the 1950s and 1960s, over the following decades migration started being more controlled between both countries. Now most of these migrants coming from Indonesia are arrested and sent back to their country of origin, where they also face economic difficulties and where the securitization of migration is also very present.

The case of Indonesia

The end of the Vietnam War in 1975 represented the victory of the communist regime, which resulted in massive outflows of Vietnamese-Chinese descendants. Back then, Malaysia, Thailand, and Indonesia were the three top destination countries in Southeast Asia for these groups seeking refuge elsewhere. The Indonesian government placed those who were arriving in a refugee processing camp at Galang Island. The international community donated money to help Indonesia in its effort to protect those escaping conflict. And the Indonesian Minister of Foreign Affairs Mochtar Kusumaatmadja made public statements acknowledging that these refugees needed protection (Lee, 2017). However, while in 1979 the term used to describe these migratory flows was that of "refugees", in the past 20 years, Indonesian leaders have referred to refugees and asylum seekers as "illegal migrants" (Lee, 2017).

Since the 1990s, the country has seen the arrival of refugees from Afghanistan and Iran because of the easiness to enter the territory and its living costs and has thus had a long tradition of hosting refugees. But in recent times, the country has shifted its policies towards immigration and has strengthened border control and made it more difficult for those seeking refuge to gain protection in the country. The world's fourth largest country by population is home to a wide range of cultures, which is even more enlarged by its role as transit and destination country. It is home to economic migrants, but it also harbors foreign victims of trafficking from abroad. Arrested unauthorized migrants, whatever their condition, are repatriated to their home countries (Missback & Palmer, 2018). And even though asylum seekers continue to arrive from different countries of origin, human rights protection for these groups is still missing.

Indonesia is therefore a home for many refugees, including the Rohingya. These groups seek refuge in the country for different reasons. Firstly, because of its location and the sovereignty of its waters, as there are many loopholes that facilitate the arrival of immigrants through waters without examination from immigration authorities. Its coastline of about 34,000 miles in length makes it hard to patrol effectively and simplifies undetected entries (Missback & Palmer, 2018). Secondly, because there is a strong presence of UNHCR and the International Organization for Migration (IOM), which helps them deal with immigration issues, especially relating to refugees and asylum seekers. And thirdly, because there are corrupt personnel that make a business of facilitating the arrival of foreign immigrants (Isa, 2017).

Indonesia is not a signatory to the 1951 Convention, but since the principle of non-refoulement is customary law and thus binding on all states, the government has argued that it follows the Refugee Convention "in spirit". That is also the reason why many foreigners arriving to the country and expressing the wish to apply for asylum were not deported, but categorized as illegal immigrants and processed through immigration regulations (Isa, 2017). In practice, many other refugee rights are overlooked, as refugees continue to be viewed through the security prism. It was not until 2000 that Article 28G(2) on the right to obtain political asylum was inserted into the 1945 Constitution of the Republic of Indonesia. It was not until the Presidential Regulation

125/2016 that a definition of refugee was established in Indonesian law, although the bill reflects the view of the government that refugees should be dealt as a security matter, and left out their rights (Sjamsoe'oed, 2019). In fact, this is even publicly acknowledged by the government, as Dicky Komar, the Director of Human Rights at the Ministry of Foreign Affairs, said, "The government has no obligation to fulfill the rights of refugees. . . . This is a temporary process, they will not stay long in Indonesia as integration is not part of our policy" (Jakarta Globe, 2017).

Adding up to this unfavorable legislation, the government has used the logic of securitization to construct the Rohingya community as an existential threat. And without taking into consideration international norms relating to the protection of refugees, it is hard for these to secure protection in countries like Indonesia and Malaysia. In the meantime, they remain undocumented migrants. And Article 85 of Indonesian Law No. 6/2011 authorizes detention of undocumented migrants for up to ten years without review. There are also no national laws prohibiting discrimination, which allows for public authorities to discriminate migrants in the country (Missbach & Palmer, 2018).

Terrorism has also contributed to furthering this negative perception of immigrants in Indonesia. Much of Indonesia's counter-terrorist legislation was adopted after the Bali bombings of October 2002, which killed 202 people (MFA, 2022). The attack consisted of the detonation of bombs by members of Jemaah Islamiyah, a violent Islamist terrorist group. Following the attacks, three of the members of the group were sentenced to death. Since the bombings, a special police unit was also designed to handle issues related to terrorism. Today, radicalization and citizens leaving for Syria to fight for the Islamic State are some of the biggest terrorist-related concerns in the country. One of the worries is precisely related to foreign fighters returning to the country and coming from other potential radicalization areas such as the southern Philippines (Missback & Palmer, 2018).

One of the responses to the terrorist attacks was the enactment of Anti-Terrorism Law No. 15/2003, which gives a rather broad definition of terrorism and authorizes the detention of suspects without trial for up to six months as well as broad powers to intercept communications. The latter powers were further reinforced and broadened in scope with the approval of Law No. 17/2011 on State Intelligence. Presidential Regulation No. 125 of 2016 is an example of this treatment of refugees in Indonesia as a security issue which, at the same time, offers little consideration to the human rights of refugees in the country. Rather than offering any durable solution, it continues declaring Indonesia as merely a transit country and creates a "permanent temporariness", failing to establish any durable solution and protection for refugees in the country (Missbach et al., 2018). In 2018, the Eradication of Criminal Acts of Terrorism Law amended the Anti-Terrorism Law of 2003 and established significant extensions to the periods for pre-charge and pre-trial detention (RSI, 2021; Soeriaatmadja, 2018). In early 2021, the National Plan of

Action on Countering Violent Extremism was initiated, with the intention to coordinate efforts to counter terrorism and control deradicalization. While the country seeks to become a regional leader in counter-extremism and counter-terrorism efforts (U.S. Department of State, 2020), their laws and practices raise issues regarding human rights compliance (RSI, 2021). There are concerns about wrongful arrests (Soeriaatmadja, 2018), the use of torture to obtain evidence (ALRC, 2016), and the accusation of innocent civilians of being terrorist and abuse of power by security forces (James, 2021).

Even in the cases when migrants use Indonesia as a transit country, they find themselves stuck in it because of lack of safe pathways. In these cases, some can be stuck for months or even years (Mohammadi & Askary, 2022). A man in this situation, tired of waiting to be resettled since 2015, set himself on fire in the streets of Medan in 2021 (Llewellyn, 2021a). Nevertheless, Indonesia still sees itself as a transit and not a destination country, which has allowed the continuity of governmental discourses denying the need to provide refugee protection.

Migration in the Oceanian region: the case of Australia

Its closeness with Australia has also made Indonesia an important transit state for those trying to make their way to Australia. Because of the large numbers of incoming refugees in this Oceanian country, the government decided to deter further migration by turning back boats with asylum seekers to other neighboring countries.

While the first joint Indonesia-Australia policing started in the 1990s and was on anti-smuggling activities, it slowly developed into a movement preventing asylum seekers from Indonesia (Kneebone et al., 2021). Since 2000, Australia has provided significant funding and other resources to Indonesia to refrain migrants from starting their journeys to migrate to Australia. The language to refer to these migratory movements has also moved from referring to them as asylum seekers to illegal immigrants (Pickering, 2004). Their bilateral cooperation developed into the Bali Process in 2002, on the basis of the Conference on People Smuggling, Trafficking in Persons and Related Transnational Crime (Kneebone, 2014), which in 2016 also became the Bali Declaration.[1]

With the expulsion of thousands of Rohingyas from Myanmar in late 2008, the Bali Process was reactivated (Kneebone, 2014) and asylum seekers from Indonesia and other regions were framed in a smuggling-trafficking discourse (Kneebone et al., 2021). These practices also turned into a new

1 For more information, see: International Labour Organization. (2016). *The Bali declaration*, APRM.16/D.6. www.ilo.org/wcmsp5/groups/public/-ed_norm/-relconf/documents/meeting-document/wcms_537445.pdf

Immigration Law (Law No. 6 of 2011). Article 119(1) makes it an offence to stay in the country without a valid document or visa, punishable by up to five years of prison.

Over time, the securitization of migration in Indonesia has been further reinforced, and since 2008 there is clear collaboration to reinforce borders with Australia (Australian Embassy, 2008). This has meant an increase of control by Indonesian forces on immigration movements, and it has also resulted in an increased propensity to detain immigrants in the country (Nethery et al., 2012). This collaboration between the two countries has also meant the externalization of Australian border control. In the words of Nethery, Rafferty-Brown, and Taylor:

> The shift towards a tougher approach to asylum seekers in Indonesia, including the extensive network and more frequent use of immigration detention, is the outcome of many years of Australian financial support and political lobbying. In doing so, Australia has exported its asylum policy for domestic political reasons. Indonesian and Australian cooperation on detention policy has been facilitated by the maturing relationship between the two countries, and the financial and diplomatic incentives that Australia has provided Indonesia.
>
> (Nethery et al., 2012)

Australia is considered one of the world's major immigration nations. By 2022, 30% of the population was born overseas, the largest countries of origin being England, India, China, and New Zealand (ABS, 2022). The number of refugees in Australia since the end of World War II passed the number of 950,000 in 2023 (RCA, 2023).

The way migration is dealt with in the country today is marked by a breaking point, when in August 2001 the Norwegian cargo ship "MV Tampa" rescued an Indonesian boat with 430 refugees, and it decided to bring them to Australian land although the nearest port embarkation was in Indonesia. The response of the then prime minister of Australia was to deny access to Tampa to its national waters. He declared, "We do not believe that we have an international legal obligation to take these people" (Reliefweb, 2001), alleging that the country has the right to refuse entry to a foreign vessel as a fundamental right of a nation's sovereignty. Evidently, the problem was not the vessel itself, but the 430 asylum seekers the ship wanted to disembark on Australian territory. The refugees were then considered a threat for the government, a threat to Australia's sovereignty, and thus a threat to its national security (Kasic, 2014).

The Australian government sent the Special Air Service (SAS) troops to control the ship and send the people in the boat to third countries, including Papua New Guinea and Nauru, which were not signatories of the 1951 Refugee Convention, meaning that the situation of these asylum seekers could even worsen. The decision of Prime Minister Howard was mostly reinforced by the media. The Daily Telegraph, for instance, wrote that "Australia should stand firm and not accept illegal immigrants" (Watson, 2008). As put by Kasic, this situation was perceived as a "moral panic" situation for Australian nationals, understood as the concern that these asylum seekers could be a threat to the values of the country or perceiving that "a cherished way of life is in jeopardy" (Kasic, 2014). It seems that the government's securitization of migration at that point was largely accepted by both the public and even the Labor Opposition (Garland, 2008; Kasic, 2014).

Since then, an operation called "Pacific Solution" was installed, designed as an externalization policy to control migration at sea and push back boats. The program had to be implemented from 2001 to 2007, but several operations on the same line have followed. "Pacific Solution" was designed to transport asylum seekers to detention centers on island nations in the Pacific Ocean. They were mostly sent to the detention centers in Nauru island and Papua New Guinea's Manus Island. Doherty (2016) said it clearly: "It is current government policy that no person who arrives in the country by boat seeking asylum . . . is ever settled in Australia". Instead, they were sent to the islands. There is evidence suggesting that Australian officials looked at the restrictive policies on asylum seekers arriving by sea of the United States and designed Pacific Solution following the same lines (Magner, 2004; Frelick et al., 2016). The result has been that of asylum seekers being left in these islands for years, some still remaining there in 2023, since their arrival ten years before (Osborne, 2023; ASRC, 2023).

Even though the policy was largely dismantled when Prime Minister John Howard left the government and was succeeded by a new government, a similar policy was again introduced in 2012 with Prime Minister Kevin Rudd. And in 2013, the Abbott government commenced Operation Sovereign Borders (OSB), which took over and became a military-led operation turning back boats carrying immigrants trying to reach Australia. In June 2023, the last refugee held by the Australian government in Nauru detention center left the facility, emptying the center for the first time in more than a decade (Morris, 2023).

The country followed a humanitarian discourse similar to that of the European Union, arguing that the intention was to save lives at sea and protect people smuggling. In reality, what evidence shows is that the country has only been trying to deter those making their way with the intent to seek asylum. And although there were already important measures to control immigration and borders, the OBS encompassed a more important military aspect. The Australian government also conducts entry-screening procedures for those arriving at their national airports. These assess whether those arriving seek to apply for asylum and return them before they can submit their applications or detain them indefinitely until they are assessed as refugees (RCA, 2021).

The response to contend migration did not just stop there. The Howard government advanced the Border Protection (Validation and Enforcement

Powers) Act 2001 and the Migration Amendment (Excision from Migration Zone) Act 2001. This is an Act "to validate the actions of the Commonwealth and the others in relation to the *MV Tampa* and other vessels, and to provide increased powers to protect Australia's borders, and for related purposes". Subsection 185(3A) states that officers can detain any person within a detained ship or aircraft, and "take the person, or cause the person to be taken, to a place outside Australia". What is more, any detention of ship, aircraft, or persons inside them, are not unlawful "and proceedings . . . may not be instituted or continued in any court against the Commonwealth". This does not only allow the use of force towards asylum seekers, but it also removes the courts from reviewing their claims (Devetak, 2007).

The detention of asylum seekers is not prohibited under international law, but it should be a measure of last resort and only in case there is a threat to "public order, public health and national security", as stated by the Guidelines of UNHCR (2012). It is for this reason that Australia has received many criticisms not only by the UN Refugee Agency, but also from other human rights organizations and NGOs (Phillips & Spinks, 2013), to the extent that a UN Working Group stated that "criminals were being treated better than asylum-seekers" (Gelber & McDonald, 2006).

With time, Australia's government has kept on broadening legislation negatively affecting refugees and asylum seekers. Section 197C of Migration and Maritime Powers Legislation Amendment (Resolving the Asylum Legacy Caseload) Act 2014 establishes non-refoulement obligations are "irrelevant to removal of unlawful non-citizens", further stating that it is "irrelevant whether Australia has non-refoulement obligations in respect of an unlawful non-citizen". Thus, officers have to remove even asylum seekers irrespective of whether this carries a breach of the principle of non-refoulement by the Australian government.

It is becoming more difficult for asylum seekers to find refuge in Australia. Following Section 46A of the Migration Act 1958, those coming in an unauthorized maritime boat will be denied their asylum or visa applications. To add more complications, Operation Sovereign Borders, a military-led border security operation established in 2013 committed to "protecting Australia's borders, combating people smuggling in our region, and preventing people from risking their lives at sea", operates under a veil of silence, lacking mechanisms of transparency or accountability (Ghezelbash et al., 2018). The government's approach in these regards has been to justify not commenting on these operations due to national security interests and because it would benefit "the people smugglers and their business model" (Chambers, 2015).

The terrorist attack of 9/11 in the United States also had strong implications for Australia's counter-terrorist strategies, even if this occurred in a place remote from the region. Australia adapted its laws focusing on issues around border control, irregular maritime migration, and terrorism (Crock & Parsons, 2023). These areas were further reinforced after the 2002 terrorist attack in Bali, Indonesia, which represented another key moment to understand the continuing securitization process of migration in the country. In this case, the event was a turning point for the role of terrorism in Australia, because even if the attack did not take place within its borders, 88 Australian nationals were killed (MFA, 2022). In a similar way, the 2005 London bombings and its subsequent legislation developments also marked the pathway for Australian reforms. After the London attacks, the Anti-Terrorism Act 2005 was enacted. This bill has been highly disputed, and so it was the Anti-Terrorism Act (No.2) 2005. A Human Rights Committee of the United Nations (2009) submitted a report on the latter, criticizing it for different reasons. Among other things, the Committee was particularly concerned about

> (a) the vagueness of the definition of terrorist act; (b) the reversal of the burden of proof contrary to the right to be presumed innocent; (c) the fact that "exceptional circumstances", to rebut the presumption of bail relating to terrorism offences, are not defined in the Crimes Act, and; (d) the expanded powers of the Australian Security Intelligence Organization (ASIO), including so far unused powers to detain persons without access to a lawyer in conditions of secrecy for up to seven-day renewable periods.

With the Anti-Terrorism Act 2005, control orders were also approved, modifying the Criminal Code Act 1995.[2] These orders are used as a surveillance tool to monitor suspect terrorists without the requirement of having committed an offence and allowing the Australian Federal Police (AFP) to monitor and restrict activities of suspects, thus limiting freedom of movement, speech, and association (Hurley, 2013). Preventive Detention Orders,[3] from the other hand, are another Australian measure to counter-terrorism. They allow officers to detail a person if they are suspected of committing a terrorist attack. These orders are approved by a judge without a trial, and no particular offence has to have occurred. Thus, it is only an order to prevent a possible future offence from happening, based on hearsay and speculation (Hurley, 2013).

With time, Australia ended up adopting anti-terrorist measures similar to those in the United States and the United Kingdom. Each year, new legislation intensified migration controls and police powers (Jupp, 2009). And since 9/11, Australia, which had no national laws dealing specifically with terrorism, has enacted more than 60 laws on the subject (Williams, 2013; Ananian-Welsh & Williams, 2014). In 2019, there were already 82 anti-terror laws, making the case of Australia of particular interest, since there has

2 See Division 104 of the Criminal Code 1995.
3 See Division 105 of the Criminal Code 1995.

been a "hyper-legislation" (Roach, 2011) of Australia's approach to securitization (Behm, 2020). Furthermore, contrary to many other developed states, Australia does not have a Charter of Rights, which can more easily lead to violations of human rights, as the country does not have sufficient safeguards against abuse of fundamental rights.

In addition to this, in the fight against terrorism countries have also made technological developments on direct surveillance of the population, stored and monitored data in numerous transactions through access to private and public-sector databases, and then searched within this data to find a matching profile to that of the terrorist suspect. Many of these technologies pose a clear threat to the privacy rights and freedoms of citizens since they allow the state to monitor the lives of all at a much closer level (Council of Europe, 2008). But these surveillance and control measures not only concern privacy rights, but they even lead to violations of human rights, including the protection against torture, the right to personal liberty and security, the right to a fair trial including the presumption of innocence, the right to respect for private and family life, the freedoms of expression and of movement, the right to an effective remedy and victims' rights to reparation following states' unlawful acts.

Border externalization has also continuously been reinforced in Australia, with measures seeking to expand the Pacific Solution under the Abbott government both in the form of new laws and policies, but also with regional plans, including agreements with other countries like Indonesia, Sri Lanka, and Malaysia, on information-sharing and reinforcement of border controls. In 2012, the government passed the Offshore Processing and Other Measures Bill, authorizing the transfer of irregular migrants by sea to Papua Guinea, where they would be indefinitely detained until their refugee claims were resolved, although these were declared unconstitutional in 2016 by the Supreme Court of Papua New Guinea (HRW, 2016).

Conclusion

While the cases of Indonesia and Malaysia are different from that of Australia, this chapter wanted to simply bring them together to study the geographically close regions of Asia and Oceania together. But as the same cases show, Indonesia and Malaysia face large incoming flows of refugees, even though they are not signatories of the 1951 Convention Relating to the Status of Refugees nor its 1967 Protocol. While the rights of migrants are already weakened in countries securitizing migration, in these two territories their human rights are even more abused. In the case of Australia, the past 20 years, and following terrorist attacks, the country has applied a series of measures contending immigration flows from the Asian region. Over time, it has become increasingly difficult for refugees and asylum seekers to find protection in Australia, and border externalization measures have nothing but progressed.

The interesting analysis resulting from the study of all these cases is that, from the one hand, it is seen that the securitization of migration takes place in countries around the world and in regions with very different historical, social, economic, and human rights contexts. From the other hand, the severity of securitizing measures may be worse where there are non-democratic governments and where there is not even an international legal framework on human rights. Nevertheless, these cases are still an example that harder securitization measures have advanced in the field of migration and in the context of national security, through arguments such as that of the protection against criminality and the terrorist threat.

References

ALRC. (2016, September 21). Submission concerning the 3rd cycle of universal periodic review of Indonesia. *Asian Legal Resource Centre*, ALRC-UPR-001-2016.

Amnesty International. (2007). Not welcome here. *Amnesty International*, ASA 28/007/2007. Retrieved January 6, 2026, from https://www.amnesty.org/en/wp-content/uploads/2021/06/asa280072007eng.pdf

Amnesty International. (2023). Malaysia strides and setbacks. *Submission to the 45th Session of the UPR Working Group*, January-February 2024, Amnesty International, ASA 28/6867/2023.

Ananian-Welsh, R., & Williams, G. (2014). Normalisation and spread of anti-terror laws in Australia. *Melbourne University Law Review*, *38*, 362–408.

Asylum Seeker Resource Centre (ASRC). (2023, June 25). Refugees evacuated from Nauru after a decade, 80 people remain in PNG. *Asylum Seeker Resource Centre*. Retrieved February 2, 2024, from https://asrc.org.au/2023/06/25/refugees-off-nauru/

Australian Bureau of Statistics (ABS). (2022). Australia's population by country of birth. *Australian Bureau of Statistics*. Retrieved November 6, 2023, from www.abs.gov.au/statistics/people/population/australias-population-country-birth/latest-release

Australian Embassy. (2008, August 6). Australian and Indonesian minister focus on border security enhancement. *Australian Embassy in Indonesia, Media Release*. Retrieved October 31, 2023, from https://indonesia.embassy.gov.au/jakt/MR08_069.html

Battacharyya, R. (2023, January 4). Rohingya refugees are departing for Southeast Asia in increasing numbers. *The Diplomat*. Retrieved November 7, 2023, from https://thediplomat.com/2023/01/rohingya-refugees-are-departing-for-southeast-asia-in-increasing-numbers/

Behm, A. (2020). *Securitisation – turning problems into threats*. The Australia Institute.

Chambers, P. (2015). The embrace of border security: Maritime jurisdiction, national sovereignty, and the geopolitics of operation sovereign borders. *Geopolitics*, *20*(2), 404–437.

Council of Europe. (2008). *Protection the right to privacy in the fight against terrorism* (Issue Paper No. 3). Commissioner for Human Rights, Council of Europe.

Crock, M., & Parsons, C. (2023). Australia as a modern migration state: Past and present. In *Background paper to the 'World Development Report 2023: Migrants, Refugees, and Societies'*. World Bank.

Devetak, R. (2007). In fear of refugees: The politics of border protection in Australia. *The International Journal of Human Rights*, *8*(1), 101–109.

Doherty, B. (2016, August 9). A short history of Nauru, Australia's duping ground for refugees. *The Guardian*. Retrieved February 2, 2024, from www.theguardian.com/world/2016/aug/10/a-short-history-of-nauru-australias-dumping-ground-for-refugees

Economist Intelligence Unit. (2023). *Democracy index 2022*. The Economist Intelligence Unit.

Freedom House. (2023a). Freedom in the world 2023. *Freedom House*. Retrieved November 3, 2023, from https://freedomhouse.org/sites/default/files/2023-03/FIW_World_2023_DigtalPDF.pdf

Freedom House. (2023b). Global freedom status. *Freedom House*. Retrieved November 3, 2023, from https://freedomhouse.org/explore-the-map?type=fiw&year=2023

Free Malaysia Today. (2022, September 6). Shut down UNHCR office in Malaysia, says security DG. *Free Malaysia Today*. Retrieved December 6, 2023, from www.freemalaysiatoday.com/category/nation/2022/09/06/shut-down-unhcr-office-in-malaysia-says-security-dg/

Frelick, B., Kysel, I., & Podkul, J. (2016). The impact of externalization of migration controls on the rights of asylum seekers and other migrants. *Journal of Migration and Human Security*, *4*(4), 190–220.

Garland, D. (2008). On the concept of moral panic. *Crime, Media, Culture*, *4*(1).

Gelber, K., & McDonald, M. (2006). Ethics and exclusion: Representations of sovereignty in Australia's approach to asylum-seekers. *Review of International Studies*, *32*(2), 269–289.

Ghezelbash, D., Moreno-Lax, V., Klein, N., & Opeskin, B. (2018). Securitization of search and rescue at sea: The response to boat migration in the Mediterranean and offshore Australia. *International and Comparative Law Quarterly*, *67*, 315–351.

Human Rights Watch (HRW). (2016). Papua new guinea: Address abuses at UN review: Make good on commitment to close manus detention center. *Human Rights Watch*.

Human Rights Watch (HRW). (2021, January). Human Rights Watch submission to the special Rapporteur's report on pushback practices and their impact on the human rights of migrants. *Human Rights Watch*.

Human Rights Watch (HRW). (2023). World report 2023: Events of 2022. *Human Rights Watch*.

Hurley, A. (2013, August 20). The need for counter-terrorism law reform. *Right Now. Human Rights in Australia*. Retrieved February 2, 2024, from http://rightnow.org.au/opinion-3/the-need-for-counter-terrorism-law-reform/

International Organization for Migration (IOM). (2023). Malaysia: Facts and figures. *International Organization for Migration*. Retrieved November 6, 2023, from www.iom.int/countries/malaysia

Isa, M. (2017). *Securitization as policy responses of Indonesia and Malaysia to resolve Rohingya refugee crisis: Comparative studies* [Master thesis, National Research University].

Jakarta Globe. (2017, July 26). Indonesia will help refugees, but 'won't host them forever, says immigration office. *Jakarta Globe*. Retrieved October 31, 2023, from https://jakartaglobe.id/context/indonesia-will-help-refugees-wont-host-forever-says-immigration-office

James, R. (2021, May 11). 'We are living in a war zone': Violence flares in West Papua as villagers forced to flee. *The Guardian*. Retrieved October 30, 2023, from www.theguardian.com/world/2021/may/11/we-are-living-in-a-war-zone-violence-flares-in-west-papua-as-villagers-forced-to-flee

Jupp, J. (2009). Immigration, the war on terror, and the British Commonwealth. In T. E. Givens, G. P. Freeman, & D. L. Leal (Eds.), *Immigration policy and security: U.S., European, and commonwealth perspectives*. Routledge.

Kasic, A. (2014). *Australia's border control: The anxiety of a nation*. Aalborg University.

Kneebone, S. (2014). The Bali process and global refugee policy in the Asia-pacific region. *Journal of Refugee Studies*, *27*, 596–618.

Kneebone, S., Missbach, A., & Jones, B. (2021). The false promise of presidential regulation no. 125 of 2016? *Asian Journal of Law and Society*, *8*(3), 431–450.

Kudo, S. (2013). Securitization of undocumented migrants and the politics of insecurity in Malaysia. *Procedia Environmental Sciences*, *17*, 947–956.

Lee, A. (2017). Forced migrants, media, and securitization: Making sense of the changing representations of transit Asylum seekers in Indonesian print media. *Journal of ASEAN Studies*, *5*(2), 75–101.

Lih Yi, B. (2015, May 13). Malaysia tells thousands of Rohingya refugees to 'go back to your country. *The Guardian*. Retrieved November 6, 2023, from www.theguardian.com/world/2015/may/13/malaysia-tells-thousands-of-rohingya-refugees-to-go-back-to-your-country

Liow, J. C. (2006). Malaysia's approach to Indonesian migrant labor: Securitization, politics or catharsis? In R. Emmers (Ed.), *Non-traditional security in Asia*. Routledge.

Llewellyn, A. (2021a). Desperate Afghan refugee sets himself on fire in Indonesia. *Al Jazeera*. Retrieved September 22, 2023, from www.aljazeera.com/news/2021/12/3/desperate-afghan-refugee-sets-himself-on-fire-in-indonesia

Magner, T. (2004). A less than 'pacific' solution for Asylum seekers in Australia. *International Journal of Refugee Law*, *16*(1).

Mahalingam, R. (2022). Securitising irregular migration, refugees, and potential security threats in Malaysia. *Malaysian Journal of Social Sciences and Humanities*, *7*(8).

May, G. (2015). Using security: The securitisation of migration in Malaysia. *The New Birmingham Review*, *2*(1), 31–41.

Migration Policy Institute (MPI). (2020). Top 25 destinations of international migrants. *Migration Policy Institute*. Retrieved November 3, 2023, from www.migrationpolicy.org/programs/data-hub/charts/top-25-destinations-international-migrants?width=1000&height=850&iframe=true

Minister for Foreign Affairs (MFA). (2022). 20th anniversary of the 2002 Bali bombings. *Minister for Foreign Affairs of Australia*. Retrieved February 10, 2024, from www.foreignminister.gov.au/minister/penny-wong/media-release/20th-anniversary-2002-bali-bombings

Missbach, A., Adiputera, Y., Prabandari, A., Cintika, G., Yudha Swatiska, F., & Raditya, D. (2018). *Stalemate: Refugees in Indonesia-presidential regulation no. 126 of 2016* (Policy Paper No. 14). Centre for Indonesian Law, Islam and Society.

Missbach, A., & Palmer, W. (2018). Indonesia: A country grappling with migrant protection at home and abroad. *Migration Policy Institute*. Retrieved September 22, 2023, from www.migrationpolicy.org/article/indonesia-country-grappling-migrant-protection-home-and-abroad

Mixed Migration Centre (MMC). (2021). *A transit country no more: Refugees and asylum seekers in Indonesia*. Author.

Mohammadi, S., & Askary, S. (2022). Refugees live in destitution in Indonesia: Years of limbo and suffering lead refugees to protests for many weeks now for resettlement. *ReliefWeb*. Retrieved September 22, 2023, from https://reliefweb.int/report/indonesia/refugees-live-destitution-indonesia-years-limbo-and-suffering-lead-refugees

Morris, J. (2023). As Nauru shows, asylum outsourcing has unexpected impacts on host communities. *Migration Policy Institute*. Retrieved February 2, 2024, from www.migrationpolicy.org/article/nauru-outsource-asylum

Nethery, A., Rafferty-Brown, B., & Taylor, S. (2012). Exporting detention: Australia-funded immigration detention in Indonesia. *Journal of Refugee Studies*, *26*(1), 88–109.

Osborne, Z. (2023, February 24). Refugees on Australian detention island sew lips shut in protest. *Al Jazeera*. Retrieved February 2, 2024, from www.aljazeera.com/news/2023/2/24/refugees-on-australian-detention-island-sew-lips-shut-in-protest

Phillips, J., & Spinks, H. (2013). *Immigration detention in Australia*. Department of Parliamentary Services, Parliament of Australia.

Pickering, S. (2004). The production of sovereignty and the rise of transversal policing: People-smuggling and federal policing. *Australian and New Zealand Journal of Criminology*, *37*, 362–379.

Refugee Council of Australia (RCA). (2021, May 19). Submission on pushback practices and their impact on the human rights of migrants. *Refugee Council of Australia*. Retrieved November 6, 2023, from www.refugeecouncil.org.au/submission-on-pushback-practices-and-their-impact-on-the-human-rights-of-migrants/

Refugee Council of Australia (RCA). (2023, May 19). Post-WW2 refugee arrivals to pass 950,000 in 2023. *Refugee Council of Australia*. Retrieved November 6, 2023, from www.refugeecouncil.org.au/950000-refugee-arrivals/

Reliefweb. (2001). Australia: Transcript of the prime minister interview with radio 2UE: Illegal immigrants. *News and Press Release, Government of Australia*. Retrieved February 2, 2024, from https://reliefweb.int/report/afghanistan/australia-transcript-prime-minister-interview-radio-2ue-illegal-immigrants

Rights and Security International (RSI). (2021). Indonesia: National security and human rights background. *Rights and Security International*. Retrieved October 30, 2023, from www.rightsandsecurity.org/assets/downloads/Indonesia_Report_Final.pdf

Roach, K. (2011). *The 9/11 effect: Comparative counter-terrorism*. Cambridge: Cambridge University Press.

Sjamsoe'oed, M. (2019, October 2). The nexus of human rights and security in Indonesia's approach to refugees. *Refugee Law Initiative's Blog*. Retrieved October 30, 2023, from https://rli.sas.ac.uk/blog/nexus-human-rights-and-security-indonesias-approach-refugees

Soeriaatmadja, W. (2018, May 24). Indonesia's improved anti-terror Bill to allow for longer detention, pre-emptive arrests. *The Straits Times*. Retrieved October 30, 2023, from www.straitstimes.com/asia/se-asia/indonesias-improved-anti-terror-bill-allows-for-longer-detention-pre-emptive-arrests

SUARAM. (2002). Human rights report 2002. *Suara Rakyat Malaysia*, p. 133.
UN DESA. (2020). International migrant stock 2020. *United Nations Department of Economic and Social Affairs, population division*. Retrieved December 1, 2023, from www.un.org/development/desa/pd/content/international-migrant-stock
United Nations High Commissioner for Refugees (UNHCR). (2012). Detention guidelines: Guidelines on the applicable criteria and standards relating to the detention of asylum-seekers and alternatives to detention. *United Nations High Commissioner for Refugees*. Retrieved November 6, 2023, from www.unhcr.org/media/unhcr-detention-guidelines
United Nations High Commissioner for Refugees (UNHCR). (2022). *Global report 2022*. Author.
United Nations High Commissioner for Refugees (UNHCR). (2023a). *Global appeal 2023: Asia and the Pacific*. Author.
United Nations High Commissioner for Refugees (UNHCR). (2023b, August 31). Desperate journeys: Rohingya refugees in search of protection. Rohingya refugees fleeing over land and sea – quarterly update. *United Nations High Commissioner for Refugees*.
UN News. (2023, January 31). IOM steps up support as Rohingya refugee numbers rise in Southeast Asia. *UN News*. Retrieved November 7, 2023, from https://news.un.org/en/story/2023/01/1133017
U.S. Department of State. (2020, June 24). *Country reports on terrorism 2019*. U.S. Department of State Bureau of Counterterrorism.
Vinothaa, S. (2022, September 8). Amnesty: M'sia insincere if UNHCR deemed 'foreign interference. *Malaysia Kini*. Retrieved December 6, 2023, from www.malaysiakini.com/news/635024
Watson, R. (2008). Permanent populism: The Howard government 1996–2007. *Australian Journal of Political Science*, *43*(3), 617–634.
Williams, G. (2013). The legal legacy of the "war on terror. *Macquarie Law Journal*, *3*, 6–7.

8

Securitizing migration in the Middle East and Africa

Migration in the Middle Eastern region: the cases of Saudi Arabia and Qatar

As introduced by the International Labor Organization (ILO), "the admission and employment system implemented by most countries in the Arab States region is based on relatively liberal entry, restricted rights and limited duration of employment contracts and visas" (ILO, 2023). The system that these countries implement is called the 'kafala system'. The kafala system is a legal framework and sponsorship program used mainly in the Gulf countries of the Middle East to employ migrant workers through a local sponsor called 'kafeel', except in Bahrain, where workers are sponsored by a governmental agency. The 'kafeel', usually the employer, is then in charge of providing the permit and all travel, housing, and transportation expenses. This system has been used in the Gulf Cooperation Countries (Bahrain, Kuwait, Oman, Qatar, Saudi Arabia, and the United Arab Emirates), Jordan, and Lebanon. Since the system falls under the jurisdiction of interior ministries and not labor ministries, workers usually have no protection under the destination country's labor law (Robinson, 2022).

Initially, the system was set up to employ Arab workers from nearby countries. But after the oil boom of the 1970s and the discovery of rich natural resources at their hands, these countries became prosperous, and there was a sudden wealth accumulated in states with rather small populations. It was a period of big growth and important infrastructure had to be built. There was then a need to turn to foreign workers to fill this construction and other needs, and a preference towards South Asian ones, as they offered cheaper labor.

The largest number of these migrant workers are part of the construction sector, but also the domestic one. An important part are female migrants. They are informal workers and because of their condition usually face further abuse. Their situation is so ill-protected that they have often been coerced by their bosses, and their jobs abroad have resulted in a variety of physical and emotional abuse, including sexual abuse (Zahrul Anam et al., 2022). In fact,

DOI: 10.4324/9781003458159-10

their situation can be so detrimental, that some countries have restricted the outflow of unskilled migrant domestic workers to Gulf countries because of their vulnerability and risks they may encounter. This has been the case of Sri Lanka and Nepal (Babar, 2021) and of Bangladesh during the 1980s and 1990s (Uddin, 2021).

Due to the FIFA World Cup that took place between November and December of 2022 in Qatar, the abuses of the kafala system became more manifested, as there was an international spotlight during the preparations of the event. More than 6,500 migrant workers from Asian countries died in Qatar since December 2010 when the country won the right to host the World Cup, as reported by *The Guardian* in 2021, although numbers could be much bigger since figures do not include numbers from many countries of origin (The Guardian, 2021). The following lines will present the cases of Saudi Arabia and Qatar, as these are two important migration countries in the region still implementing the kafala system. Although the context is much different from that of other regions, these cases hopefully will be helpful to understanding the link between migration and security in the Middle Eastern region.

The Kingdom of Saudi Arabia is the largest Arab country. With a total population of about 36 million (World Bank, 2022), more than 13 million are foreigners coming from countries such as India, Indonesia, Pakistan, Bangladesh, Egypt, Syria, and Yemen (IHD, 2023; The New Arab, 2023). The country hosts the second largest migrant population in absolute numbers (Lysa, 2022). Most of these migrants arrive to the country as migrant workers looking for economic opportunities. The country is the destination point of the Eastern Migration Route, one of the most crowded maritime migratory routes in the world.

But when studying securitization practices in the field of migration in this country, one needs to go back to the 1990s. After the 1991 Gulf War, there was social unrest and general discontent. With Prince Na'ef, Saudi Arabia began politicizing immigration and started nationalizing the labor market through "Saudization" policies (Thiollet, 2021). He reformed the kafala system and authorized raids in working spaces to control the legal status of immigrant workers. It was not until the 2000s that Prince Abdallah, the ruler of the country, developed measures to counter international terrorism and started moving towards redressing the worsening socioeconomic situation (Jones, 2003). After years of new programs by the Ministry of Labour to push for economic incentives and immigration control reforms, and important reconfigurations of the executive branch, the country has built negative sentiments towards migrants, as Saudization policies have always aimed at boosting employment of Saudi nationals, even though immigration rates have not stopped growing.

Saudi Arabia is a non-signatory state to the Refugee Convention, and it has no domestic refugee law, which means that its refugee population are generally not recognized as such. In practice, those who are likely to qualify for refugee status are considered foreign workers (Lysa, 2022). In recent years, several immigration policies to further control immigration have been introduced – even if not directed to those seeking for asylum specifically. Since 2006, the Immigration and Passports Service has kept files of irregular migrants who have overstayed their visas. In 2014, fingerprinting female foreign workers became mandatory, and the following year biometric submission was also mandatory for the children of immigrants, just to mention a few examples. The Ministry of Interior has undertaken campaigns to correct the status of undocumented workers in the country, which led to mass deportations for many. In July 2023, new penalties were included for those private entities employing irregular migrants and thus violating the Saudi Residency Law of 1952. Penalties include one-year imprisonments for managers of these businesses, and deportation if managers are expatriates. Aiding foreign nationals entering the kingdom and employing, aiding, or sheltering immigrants who have entered illegally or have overstayed their visas is also punishable by law.

In recent episodes of extreme violence, Saudi border guards shot hundreds of Ethiopians trying to cross the border from Yemen into the kingdom (Adams, 2023; Mills et al., 2023; MMC, 2023). According to Human Rights Watch and the United Nations, this has been a practice used for several months, as it accused the Saudi government of killing hundreds of refugees and asylum seekers, including women and children, who were trying to cross the Yemen-Saudi border between March 2022 and June 2023 (HRW, 2023a; UN, 2022). The organization identified vehicles with heavy machine guns, mortar projectiles, and other explosive weapons at guards' positions at the border as well as other expanding border security infrastructure (HRW, 2023b). Mass pushbacks of Ethiopian refugees and migrants by Saudi Arabian forces have also occurred at the border, thus ignoring individual assessment of the right to seek asylum and the principle of non-refoulement, leaving these migrants to their fate and at risk of facing persecution or threat to their lives at home (HRW, 2023b).

In March 2021, the Saudi government announced a series of changes to the kafala system to ease restrictions and allow migrant workers covered by the labor law to change jobs without the consent of their employer. Likewise, under certain conditions, if a worker wants to terminate the employment relationship and leave the country, it no longer needs the employer's approval which was required before. Migrant workers will still need to submit a request to the government to leave the country, but they are not required to have the employer's permission. Nevertheless, domestic workers, home guards, private drivers, and farmers – some of the most vulnerable groups under the kafala system – are not included in the reforms and must therefore still get permission from their employers to quit or change jobs. That is why while NGOs have welcomed new labor reforms, they are still concerned that they are insufficient as the kafala system is still an exploitative one (BHRRC, 2021). Human Rights Watch (HRW, 2023c) still considers the kafala system implemented by Saudi Arabia as one of the most restrictive and abusive ones in the region, despite recent reforms.

The case of Qatar is not so different from its neighboring state. Qatar is a country of a population of almost 2.7 million people (World Bank, 2022). Of these, only 300,000 of its residents are citizens, with the remainder being migrant workers from Asia and Africa (Campbell, 2022; Bouri, 2023). Some countries in the region have undergone important changes regarding their kafala systems in recent years. In light of being the host to the 2022 World Cup, Qatar attempted to address some of the human rights affairs concerning migrant workers. One of the moves towards this direction was to allow the ILO to open an office in Doha in 2018 and abolish the kafala system (Bouri, 2023). The country has undergone labor reforms and now allows these immigrants to change jobs and leave the country without employers' permission (Ioanes, 2022; HRW, 2017). However, there is still an implementation problem, and the system continues to operate in practice (HRC, 2020; Bouri, 2023). In fact, shortly after labor reforms preceding the World Cup, migrant workers building venues for the event were working long hours in hard conditions and without rest days, leading to at least about 500 of these laborers dying as a result, as stated by the Secretary General of Qatar's World Cup Organizing Committee (Campbell, 2022). Furthermore, very often these reforms exclude domestic workers, who are still the most vulnerable within the kafala system (Alobaid, 2021).

For example, Law No. 13 of 2018 cancels all requirements for migrant workers to get permission to leave their employers or leave Qatar. But not all workers were covered by the law. It was not until Decision No. 95 of 2019 that domestic workers, workers in government and public institutions, and those employed in the oil, gas, and agriculture sectors, could also leave without a permit from their employer. Nonetheless, domestic workers are still required to provide a 72-hour notice to their employer before leaving their employment or leaving Qatar. If they fail to provide such notice, they may lose their chance to claim unpaid wages or even face a four-year travel ban to Qatar. These decisions have made it easier in theory to leave one's working place. However, it is still hard for migrants to leave due to Law No. 21 of 2015, which states that employers can retain travel documents of migrant workers if the latter consents in writing. While the law prohibits confiscation of migrant workers' documentation, allowing employers to retain these documents can end up in abuse. Cancelling workers' residency permits and filing false absconding charges are other practices used by employers to retaliate migrant workers who want to leave their jobs (ILO, 2023). Thus, in practice it is still difficult to make the decision to leave to another place.

The Special Rapporteur on contemporary forms of racism, racial discrimination, xenophobia, and related intolerance reported in 2020 that "immense power imbalances persist between employers and migrant workers" rooted in the kafala system (HRC, 2020). An example of this is that domestic workers still require exit permits to leave the country and migrant workers must wait five years before transferring employers if their contract does not specify a duration.

On the other hand, while Qatar has still not ratified the Convention Relating to the Status of Refugees of 1951 and its 1967 Protocol, the country has been the first in its region to pass a law on political asylum. Law No. 11 of 2018 on the Regulation of the Political Asylum guarantees access to a range of governmental free services. The definition of 'refugee' is quite limited in its scope and there is "immense discretion granted in the Law to the Ministry of the Interior and the Prime Minister". This is because there are provisions stating that not issuing a response to an asylum petition constitutes a rejection of such application, or because asylum seekers and refugees can be deported if they engage in political activity of a country of the Minister of Interior's choosing (CERD, 2019).

Migration in the African region: the case of South Africa

South Africa used to be known to have one of the most welcoming and safeguarding refugee systems. It has also ratified without reservations the 1951 Refugee Convention Relating to the Status of Refugees and the 1969 OAU Convention Governing the Specific Aspects of Refugee Problems. In the migration history of South Africa, the country has been known to welcome big refugee waves fleeing from armed conflicts and civil wars in the continent and seeking protection in this country.

However, since 2011 there has been a significant drop in the numbers of forced migrants compared to the first ten years of the millennium. Migration is still an important phenomenon in the African continent, though, and it will continue to be as long as political conflicts and environmental change continue hitting the continent. In the South Africa region in particular, migration is mostly driven for economic reasons, political instability, and environmental hazards. South Africa has been the top destination country in the continent for the past years, with about 2.9 million migrants (ACSS, 2023). But as South Africa used to be open to refugees, in the past years its policies have shifted mostly to refrain incoming economic migration and refugees in the country. The patterns that are seen in the past couple of decades in the southern region of Africa are characterized by the reluctancy to allow the free movement of economic migrants. As a result, new restrictions have been implemented such as stronger border controls to refrain further incoming migration flows.

The South African legislation on international migration is based on the 1999 White Paper on International Migration and implemented through the

Immigration Act of 2002, the Refugees Act of 1998, and the Border Management Authority Act of 2020. Both laws have been amended in recent years under the lead of the Department of Home Affairs, and new bills have been passed to address more recent migration movements and gaps in legislation. This has meant a series of changes in the way migrants are accepted and treated in the country. More restrictions have been established, such as the reinforcement of borders, but other difficulties have also been imposed, such as bureaucratic burdens to obtaining asylum seeker permits to move freely within the country and exercise other basic rights.

Immigration was tackled as the Apartheid lasted, selecting newcomers that fulfilled certain preferred requirements, such as being white or from European culture. However, after the Apartheid, and while the African National Congress wanted to guide the population towards new non-discriminatory standards, immigration patterns changed and so did the laws of the country. Nevertheless, those preferred immigrants were still chosen according to certain particularities, such as being skilled migrants.

In the post-Apartheid period, South Africa ratified some international human rights treaties including the 1951 Geneva Convention Relating to the Status of Refugees, the 1967 New York Protocol relating to the Status of Refugees, as well as other regional instruments such as the 1969 Convention Governing the Specific Aspects of Refugee Problems in Africa (which is an OAU Convention). Nationally, the legal framework regarding refugees is based on the Refugees Act 130 of 1998 (hereafter RA 1998), which was a progressive law at the time which put the country at the forefront of refugee protection within the region. Since then, the refugee system became an advanced, modern, and tolerant one, outstanding within the continent. The law was amended through the Refugees Amendment Act 11 of 2017 (hereafter RAA 2017), which entered into force in 2020. As a result, the refugee system of South Africa has substantially and detrimentally been altered. There are now more difficulties to access the system as there are new prescreening procedures and wider grounds to refuse the renewal of permits, such as refusal to issue those who have delayed their applications (Ziegler, 2020). Section 28(1) further declares that refugees and asylum seekers can be removed from South Africa "on grounds of national security, national interest or public order". Since there is no definition of these grounds, wide interpretations of their meanings may lead to extensive detentions and removals. Such legislative changes and introduction of restrictions have been characterized by a shift towards a security-oriented model by the Department of Home Affairs (Duncan, 2020), which in turn gives "excessive emphasis on security in government policy" in justification of responding to the terrorist threat (Hobden, 2020).

The Department of Home Affairs has maintained that an individual is an illegal migrant even if she is an asylum seeker and has applied for asylum in the country. Some are even detained before they can make their applications while already being in South Africa. Others are detained just after crossing the border. Detentions[1] are a common action related to immigration in the country, reinforcing the idea that securitization in these matters is now common in the country. As Amit (2013) states, "The framing of migration as a security threat has created a perception that the legal demands of detainees lack legitimacy, encouraging immigration officials to deny detained individuals' access to their legal rights to appeal and review".

Africa is a continent that has also suffered from the disasters of terrorism. Kenya has endured numerous terrorist attacks, Nigeria has long been dealing with the violence held by Boko Haram, Mali has seen the brutality of terrorist groups against national and international security forces, spilling over to countries like Burkina Faso and Niger. Lamentably, terrorism and its violence have also been part of the history of Africa. That is why today it is not rare to see legislation on countering terrorism advancing in the countries of this region. Particularly, South Africa's involvement in fighting against terrorism throws back to the 2013 Westgate Mall attack in Kenya (USDS, 2018). After the attack, the country started developing new legislation and bodies to protect from the terrorist threat. Among its existing measures, there is the Protection of Constitutional Democracy Against Terrorist and Related Activities Act (POCDATARA) and the Regulation of Foreign Military Assistance Act of 1998. The country also counts on the South African Police Service (SAPS) and inside it, the Crimes Against the State (CATS) Unit, among other agencies directed to identify challenges at the borders related to migration and defending the nation against crimes and terrorist offences.

The Special Rapporteur on the promotion and protection of human rights and fundamental freedoms while countering terrorism, Martin Scheinin, affirmed in a 2007 report that

> through discussions with numerous government and non-government interlocutors, it became clear that in South Africa many see the risk of terrorism primarily as coming from foreigners and that among authorities there is a temptation to bypass procedural and substantive human rights standards when dealing with foreigners unlawfully in the country.
>
> (Scheinin, 2007)

However, South Africa's role in securitizing migration is not directly linked to the fight against terrorism. As seen in most Western countries, governments have defended measures to control immigration as a way to prevent the entrance of possible terrorist fighters and possible attacks against the nation and its citizens. Their discourses have been filled with connections between migration and terrorism, and in the last years they have justified

1 Allowed by Article 34 of the Immigration Act of 2002.

the application of extraordinary measures with arguments about the need to defend the nation against the terrorist threat. Nevertheless, South Africa's securitization of migration is more connected to its history of incoming asylum seekers from neighboring countries and problems of integration, than considering the arrival of these persons as a potential terrorist peril. This does not mean that terrorism is not part of the reasons to securitize migration for the South African government, but it is not the main justification.

The White Paper on International Migration of 2017[2] sets out a framework defining the line that migration management should take in the country. White Papers are policy documents drawn by the government which are used as proposals to set up a policy framework for future legislation. Released in 2017, this White Paper on migration introduces a series of changes regarding permanent residency, citizenship, the asylum system, and other immigration related issues. While the document recognizes that immigration in the country may be beneficial in some cases, it also links migration to security risks, trafficking, and corruption (Scalabrini, 2019).

The Department of Home Affairs now follows the risk-based approach established by the White Paper on International Migration, which seeks to keep security threats out of the country because "immigration that is not managed through a risk-based approach is poorly managed immigration". The White Paper's executive summary states that the current migration system of the country "serves to perpetuate irregular migration, which in turn leads to unacceptable levels of corruption, human rights abuse and national security risks". It further states that South Africa has become an attractive destination for illegal immigrants "who pose a security threat to the economic stability and sovereignty of the country".

But the White Paper on International Migration has not been the only normative element to be developed recently. Through the Border Management Authority Act of 2020, South Africa's borders are now reinforced and managed by a new armed service, the Border Management Authority (BMA). This unit is in charge of dealing with the arrival of irregular migrants and asylum seekers at the border. The creation of these armed forces adds to the set of measures that the South African government has passed to reinforce this securitization approach to migration management (Landau & Kihato, 2017). Some commentators have noted that the Border Management Act shares many similarities with some of the securitization measures on immigration developed by the European Union which could result in a new paradigm where "millions will be detained in facilities across Africa or condemned to die along land and water borders" (Landau & Kihato, 2017).

2 *White Paper on International Migration for South Africa*, 28 July 2017, No. 41009, Department of Home Affairs of South Africa.

In November 2023, South Africa's government designed the latest White Paper on Migration titled "White Paper on Citizenship, Immigration and Refugee Protection: Towards A Complete Overhaul of the Migration System in South Africa", which is by the time of writing under public consultation. In a press statement, the Minister of Home Affairs, Aaron Motsoaledi, defended that South Africa should withdraw from the 1951 Refugee Convention and its Protocol and re-accede with reservations (Motsoaledi, 2023). It frames immigration in the country as a "crisis" and argues that legislative gaps are the source of xenophobia in the country, as these result in clashes between nationals and foreigners. If this latest version of the White Paper is approved, South Africa will move further away from human rights standards in the field of migration, and get closer to a nationalistic system.

Along with these legislative changes, there have also been movements in the streets against migration. Back in 2015, Operation Fiela was carried out to conduct raids to arrest irregular migrants in the country. One of many examples was when the police detained 235 immigrants in the Central Methodist Church of Johannesburg, where they took shelter. Following the arrests, President Zuma stated that "the government will not tolerate illegal immigrants" (NWI, 2023). In 2023, DHA immigration officials and police officers continue detaining illegal foreigners at their discretion instead of following a case-by-case approach. These practices result in unlawful arrests and detentions, disregarding the provisions of the Immigration Act and the Refugees Act.

All these changes have led some scholars to believe that there is an existing pattern in South Africa to securitize migration.[3] Ncumisa Willie, research advisor of the South African Human Rights Commission, contends, "The first amendment which shows South Africa is moving towards a more securitized approach to migration took place in 2011 and made access to refugee asylum system difficult for refugees and asylum seekers" (SAHRC, 2018). The consecutive amendments to the Immigration Act, which have also affected the Refugees Act, have led to a securitization of migration that has reduced the rights of refugees and asylum seekers in the country (Ngalo, 2018).

The case of South Africa shows again that the securitization of migration does not only appear in countries which have had to protect themselves from the terrorist threat. Securitization practices in this field have become rather common in a wide range of countries and following different ideas. It then becomes evident that terrorism is not the only event connecting migration to security. Still, the need to protect national security from the 'security threat' posed by migration remains a persistent concern to governments.

3 To read more on this, see for instance the work of Anne Hammerstad or Ncumisa Willie.

Conclusion

The cases of Saudi Arabia and Qatar in the Middle East are interesting as the migratory flows analyzed are in a particular situation. In these cases, the immigrant population are not refugees or asylum seekers, but are mostly migrant workers looking for job opportunities abroad. It is then difficult to compare the treatment of migration in these countries, as the type of migration that they are receiving is different from that which other states are struggling so much to contend. In these cases, immigration is welcome as manpower is needed. However, it is the way in which these migrants are treated whilst in the country that matters for the purposes of securitization analysis. As has been exposed, there are often no domestic laws or very few ones regarding refugees. And while changes to the kafala system have been announced more recently, in practice these are still restrictive and abusive towards immigrant workers.

On the other hand, South Africa faces a different situation. This is a country with a history of welcoming refugees during the 1990s, but which has shifted its policies in the past years in order to contend the entrance of asylum seekers and refugees within its territory. The Department of Home Affairs follows a risk-based approach to keep 'security threats' – immigration – out of the country. Intolerance towards immigration in political discourses has spread, and this has also been reflected in the streets of South Africa. Sadly, migration has become strongly securitized in the case of South Africa, showing once again that these practices are becoming rather common in countries around the world.

References

ACSS. (2023, January 9). African migration trends to watch in 2023. *Africa Center for Strategic Studies*. Retrieved November 13, 2023, from https://africacenter.org/spotlight/african-migration-trends-to-watch-in-2023/

Adams, P. (2023, August 21). Hundreds of migrants killed by Saudi border guards – report. *BBC News*. Retrieved October 26, 2023, from www.bbc.com/news/world-middle-east-66545787

Alobaid, M. (2021, September 3). The middle Eastern consensus on the Kafala system. *University of Pennsylvania Carey Law School*. Retrieved October 26, 2023, from www.law.upenn.edu/live/blogs/99-the-middle-eastern-consensus-on-the-kafala-system

Amit, R. (2013). Security rhetoric and detention in South Africa. *Forced Migration Review*, *44*.

Babar, Z. (2021). Purveyors of dreams: Labour recruiters in the Pakistan to Saudi Arabia migration corridor. *Migration and Development*, *10*(1), 68–85.

Business and Human Rights Resource Centre (BHRRC). (2021). *Saudi Arabia: Rights groups say kafala (sponsorship) system reforms fall short on freedom of movement*. Author. Retrieved November 13, 2023, from www.business-humanrights.org/en/latest-news/reforms-to-saudis-sponsorship-kafala-system-and-rights-groups-say-these-reforms-are-not-adequate/

Bouri, C. (2023, September 17). The Kafala system is facilitating labor abuses in the Middle East. *Lawfare*. Retrieved November 13, 2023, from www.lawfaremedia.org/article/the-kafala-system-is-facilitating-labor-abuses-in-the-middle-east

Campbell, C. (2022, December 16). It's rare to see change happen at this pace". A global backlash is forcing Qatar to treat migrant workers better. *Time Magazine*. Retrieved November 13, 2023, from https://time.com/6240955/qatar-world-cup-migrants-labor-reforms/

CERD. (2019, January 2). Concluding observations on the combined seventeenth to twenty-first periodic reports of Qatar. *Committee on the Elimination of Racial Discrimination* (CERD/C/QAT/CO/17-21). Retrieved November 16, 2023, from https://www.ohchr.org/en/documents/concluding-observations/cerdcqatco17-21-concluding-observations-combined-seventeenth

Duncan, J. (2020, January 20). South Africa's emerging Department of Homeland Security. *Daily Maverick*. Retrieved November 16, 2023, from www.dailymaverick.co.za/article/2020-01-20-south-africas-emerging-department-of-homeland-security/

The Guardian. (2021, February 23). Revealed: 6,500 migrant workers have died in Qatar since World Cup awarded. *The Guardian*. Retrieved October 28, 2023, from www.theguardian.com/global-development/2021/feb/23/revealed-migrant-worker-deaths-qatar-fifa-world-cup-2022

Hobden, C. (2020, February 5). South Africa takes fresh steps to restrict rights of refugees. *The Conversation*. Retrieved November 14, 2023, from https://theconversation.com/south-africa-takes-fresh-steps-to-restrict-rights-of-refugees-130606

HRC. (2020, June 13–July 3). Report of the Special Rapporteur on contemporary forms of racism, racial discrimination, xenophobia and related intolerance. *Human Rights Council*, Forty-Fourth Session, A/HRC/44/57/Add.1.

HRW. (2017, October 27). Qatar: Implementation will be key for labor reforms. *Human Rights Watch*. Retrieved October 28, 2023, from www.hrw.org/news/2017/10/27/qatar-implementation-will-be-key-labor-reforms

HRW. (2023a, August 21). Saudi Arabia: Mas killings of migrants at Yemen border. *Human Rights Watch*. Retrieved November 7, 2023, from www.hrw.org/news/2023/08/21/saudi-arabia-mass-killings-migrants-yemen-border

HRW. (2023b). They fired on us like rain. *Human Rights Watch*. Retrieved November 7, 2023, from www.hrw.org/report/2023/08/21/they-fired-us-rain/saudi-arabian-mass-killings-ethiopian-migrants-yemen-saudi

HRW. (2023c). World report 2023: Saudi Arabia. *Human Rights Watch*. Retrieved November 13, 2023, from www.hrw.org/world-report/2023/country-chapters/saudi-arabia#2c4b68

IHD. (2023). Country profiles: Saudi Arabia. *Integral Human Development*. Retrieved November 7, 2023, from https://migrants-refugees.va/country-profile/saudi-arabia/

ILO. (2022, November). What has changed for migrant workers in Qatar? *International Labour Organization*. Retrieved November 7, 2023, from www.ilo.org/infostories/en-GB/Stories/Country-Focus/world-cup-qatar#landing

ILO. (2023, November). Labour migration in the Arab States. *International Labour Organization*. Retrieved November 13, 2023, from www.ilo.org/beirut/areasofwork/labour-migration/WCMS_514910/lang-en/index.htm

Ioanes, E. (2022, November 26). Qatar's migrant labor system is bigger than the World Cup. *Vox*. Retrieved October 26, 2023, from www.vox.com/world/2022/11/26/23468456/qatar-migrant-labor-world-cup-kafala

Jones, T. (2003). Seeking a 'social contract' for Saudi Arabia. *Middle East Report, 228*(Fall). Retrieved November 8, 2023, from https://merip.org/2003/09/seeking-a-social-contract-for-saudi-arabia/

Landau, L., & Kihato, C. (2017, July 5). Securitising Africa's borders is bad for migrants, democracy, and development. *The New Humanitarian*. Retrieved November 14, 2023, from www.thenewhumanitarian.org/opinion/2017/07/05/securitising-africa-s-borders-bad-migrants-democracy-and-development

Lysa, C. (2022). Governing refugees in Saudi Arabia (1948–2022). *Refugee Survey Quarterly, 42*(1), 1–28.

Mills, A., Negeri, T., & Pavicic, M. (2023, August 22). Saudi border guards killed hundreds of Ethiopian migrants, HRW says. *Reuters*. Retrieved November 7, 2023, from www.reuters.com/world/middle-east/saudi-border-guards-killed-hundreds-ethiopian-migrants-hrw-says-2023-08-21/

Motsoaledi, A. (2023, November 12). Press statement on the release of the white paper on citizenship, immigration and refugee protection: Towards a complete overhaul of the migration system in South Africa. *Department of Home Affairs of the Republic of South Africa*. www.dha.gov.za/index.php/statements-speeches/1724-press-statement-on-the-release-of-the-white-paper-on-citizenship-immigration-and-refugee-protection-towards-a-complete-overhaul-of-the-migration-system-in-south-africa

MMC. (2023, July 5). Murderous border controls: The mass killings of Ethiopian migrants along the Saudi Arabian – Yemen border. *Mixed Migration Centre*. Retrieved November 7, 2023, from https://mixedmigration.org/articles/murderous-border-controls-ethiopian-migrants/

The New Arab. (2023, June 1). Foreigners makeup over 40% of Saudi population, census shows. *The New Arab*. Retrieved November 7, 2023, from www.newarab.com/news/foreigners-make-over-40-saudi-population-census-show

Ngalo, A. (2018, June 26). SA legislation on migrants takes wrong path. *Daily Maverick*. Retrieved November 16, 2023, from www.dailymaverick.co.za/article/2018-06-26-sa-legislation-on-migrants-takes-wrong-path/

NWI. (2023). Operation Fiela: Raids illegal immigrants. *New World Immigration*. Retrieved November 16, 2023, from www.nwivisas.com/nwi-blog/south-africa/operation-fiela-raids-illegal-immigrants/

Robinson, K. (2022, November 18). What is the kafala system? *Council on Foreign Relations*. Retrieved October 26, 2023, from www.cfr.org/backgrounder/what-kafala-system

SAHRC. (2018). SA legislation on migrants takes wrong path. *South African Human Rights Commission*. Retrieved November 14, 2023, from www.sahrc.org.za/index.php/sahrc-media/news/item/1416-sa-legislation-on-migrants-takes-wrong-path

Scalabrini. (2019). What is the White paper on international migration? *Scalabrini Centre of Cape Town*. Retrieved November 14, 2023, from www.scalabrini.org.za/news/what-is-the-white-paper-on-international-migration/

Scheinin, M. (2007). Report of the special rapporteur on the promotion and protection of human rights and fundamental freedoms while countering terrorism: Addendum. *Human Rights Council*, A/HRC/4/26/Add.1. Retrieved November 14, 2023, from https://digitallibrary.un.org/record/595030

Thiollet, H. (2021). Migrants and monarchs: Regime survival, state transformation and migration politics in Saudi Arabia. *Third World Quarterly, 43*(7), 1645–1665.

Uddin, M. A. (2021). The plight of the Bangladeshi women migrants in the middle East. *Journal of South Asian and Middle Eastern Studies*, 44(2), 66–94.

UN. (2022, October 3). Mandates of the special rapporteur on extrajudicial, summary or arbitrary executions; The Working Group on Arbitrary Detention; The Special Rapporteur on the human rights of migrants; The Special Rapporteur on trafficking in persons, especially women and children; The Special Rapporteur on violence against women and girls, its causes and consequences and the Working Group on discrimination against women and girls. *United Nations*, AL SAU 9/2022. Retrieved November 7, 2023, from https://spcommreports.ohchr.org/TMResultsBase/DownLoadPublicCommunicationFile?gId=27562

USDS. (2018, September 19). Country reports on terrorism 2017-South Africa. *United States Department of State*. Retrieved November 14, 2023, from www.refworld.org/docid/5bcf1f8021.html

World Bank. (2022). Population, total. *World Bank*. Retrieved November 7, 2023, from https://data.worldbank.org/indicator/SP.POP.TOTL

Zahrul Anam, M., Maksum, A., Musa Harahap, A., Rahmadhanitya, M. A. D., & Abdilla, M. F. (2022). Securitization of migration and kafala system towards Indonesian female migrant domestic workers in the gulf countries. *Proceedings of the International Conference on Sustainable Innovation on Humanities, Education, and Social Sciences*, *710*, 914–933.

Ziegler, R. (2020). Access to effective refugee protection in South Africa: Legislative commitment, policy realities, judicial rectifications? *Constitutional Court Review*, *10*, 65–106.

Conclusions

A more humanitarianism approach on migration

By the end of 2020, it was calculated that 184 million people lived outside of their country of origin, and about 20% of them were refugees (World Bank, 2023). Today, more than half of refugees originate from just three countries: the Syrian Arab Republic (6.5 million), Afghanistan (6.1 million), and Ukraine (5.9 million) (UNHCR, 2023a). In addition, there were more than 85,000 arrivals by sea to Italy, Greece, Spain, Cyprus, and Malta in the first half of 2023 alone (UNHCR, 2023b), including over 3,000 deaths and disappearances during these journeys through the Mediterranean (IOM, 2024). Thousands of others are fleeing from conflict every day, looking for a safe haven.

Conflicts around the world always involve migratory movements, either with internal displacements or with people fleeing their home countries searching for safety elsewhere. As a response to these migratory flows, immigration legislation and policies have harshened globally, making it more difficult for these groups to settle at destination countries. These migrants are in very vulnerable positions, and having their rights restrained once leaving their homes only increases their insecurity and changes of integration within the host country. Today, migration is approached through the lens of national security. Terrorist attacks, economic recession, in sum, and times of crisis have paved the way for politicians to justify harder security measures, not only restricting the rights of its own citizens at times, but also restricting specifically those of non-nationals in their territories.

This is a sign that the state is more concerned with national security than human security. This is important to highlight because of the changes that the international order is going through, as this will cause a direct impact on the individual. Instead of placing the person at the center of concern, the state remains the main element to be protected. We have not been able to take a more universalist approach to aim for the protection of all human beings and the international community. If there were a time in which international cooperation seemed to go towards this direction, it has not really

DOI: 10.4324/9781003458159-11

been able to succeed at this desire. Thence instead of going beyond a state-centric world politics in which each state is responsible only of the security of its sovereignty, territory, and population, we have remained right there. And while migration is also part of the international debate, it has often been dealt with at the state level. We have seen mass refugee flows around the world, and yet many states have been resistant to accept asylum seekers into their countries for considering them a potential terrorist threat, a criminal menace, an economic burden, or else. And an international response has not been appropriately given.

Bigo and Tsoukala (2008) contend that the aftermath of the War on Terror resulted in an "aestheticization of the political", understood as the obligation to "choose who the enemy is and to declare it publicly". For them, securitization practices were no longer an exception, but were in fact becoming everyday practices conceptualizing an "(in) securitization process". Through language, but also using technologies, some objects – or subjects, in the case of migration – are presented under a logic of surveillance and control. Political use of this language has led to thinking that the only way to deal with migrants is to do so through the lens of security. Therefore, the process results in a consolidation of different insecurities which are presented as global threats.

The connection between migration and security was consolidated after the events of September 11 in Western states, and it has been reinforced over time through the Bali bombings, the Mombasa and Kenya attacks, or those in European countries. These events have reinforced the imaginary of the foreigner as a potential terrorist, as discourses have blamed immigrants for important contemporary security threats. This has led to many states adopting laws and policies dealing with migration through the lens of national security, underpinning the need to protect from these external dangers threatening the nation. These laws and policies securitizing migration further manifest a perception of insecurity is spread, and that the way states deal with migration through the lens of security is a social construction, used to advance a series of measures uplifting national security.

However, as the analysis of the practical cases shows, securitization practices have spread around the globe and have not necessarily been a direct result of the events of September 11 or the Global War on Terror. In the second part of the book, practical experiences of countries in the Americas, the European Union, Asia, Oceanian, the Middle East, and Africa in the field of migration and security have been used to gain insight into the ways the securitization of migration has been carried out in different contexts. The result shows an international system that fails to deal with migration through a humanitarianism approach. First, the selected cases show a consistent practice securitizing migration which establishes a nexus between migration and national security. Second, this also demonstrates that there is a generalized prioritization for national security concerns instead of finding common solutions to international problems through multilateralism. States are dealing with what they consider *international* security threats mostly at the *domestic* level. Third, the century has brought a new wave of securitization measures which started with the events of 9/11 in the United States, and which has followed a process of diffusion and has expanded in other Western nations, not just in the European Union but also in other countries like Australia. What started as a series of mechanisms to control the terrorist threat in the US, then spread through other Western countries in the aftermath of terrorist attacks.

The panorama that we see today is one where the securitization of migration has become a consistent practice for many states around the globe. And what these practices show is that the securitization of migration has been implemented in a wide range of countries and in a wide range of contexts, thus following a logic that does not necessarily connect to the terrorist threat. Today migration is securitized in a wide range of states following different logics beyond the contention of the terrorist threat. However, what is common in all the analyzed cases is that in all instances, there is a reasoning based on the protection of national security. That leads to the fourth result, which is that these practices are another sign and evidence of the setback of the international liberal order and a reversal of liberal values.

The selected cases have been chosen according to their weight on dealing with migration in their own regions, whether that is by receiving or exporting migration, although more focus has been brought to states receiving large migration numbers. That is because these are precisely the ones that can be used as a better example to show how states manage immigration as an external security threat, and thus analyze the laws and policies they have approved establishing this link between the two spheres. All the analyzed cases are of course different. They all have different types of immigration, and they have different historical, social, and economic contexts. This makes every case unique in its own way. Therefore, these are important variables to consider when comparing them, and it must be understood that every country offers its own results. However, what this book seeks to humbly show is that there has been a kind of spill-over effect of securitization measures, which has spread practices securitizing migration across countries and regions. Securitization is not only a phenomenon of Western countries and consequence of the Global War on Terror. The securitization of migration has expanded in all regions the past 20 years, with few exceptionalities. Thus, when new security measures are adopted in a group of countries or within a region, this can easily lead to other states in other areas following with similar behaviors. And when states struggle dealing with migration, this creates the perfect context for them to impulse the justification and adoption of more measures featuring more border and migration control.

Again, what this shows is that states are still more concerned with national security than human security. And instead of moving beyond a state-centric world politics in which the state is responsible mostly to secure its sovereignty, territory, and population, we have remained right there. The multilateralist view of the liberal order, based on multilateral cooperation, international peace and security, the spread of democracy, and the protection of the human rights of all individuals has been sidelined. And as millions of refugees are escaping from conflict, countries are worried about contending these migratory flows by reinforcing their frontiers.

The rise of far-right parties has spread discourses of racism, discrimination, and xenophobia. The West has repeatedly presented the image of a male national from Arab and Muslim-majority countries as one of menace. Immigration has been considered as a potential terrorist threat. It has been blamed for economic burdens, or the scarcity of resources. However, what the Russian-Ukrainian conflict shows is that European countries responded quickly welcoming refugees resulting from the war. Paradoxically, refugees from Syria have found barriers to reach European territory. Ukrainian refugees have not been presented as security threats (Townsend, 2022), even when the Ukrainian invasion resulted into the fastest refugee crisis in the world since 1950 (Aragó, 2022). The conflict has somehow manifested a "selective empathy on refugees" (Saifi, 2022), proving that the securitization of migration is nothing but the result of a social construction.

The construction of the 21st century world order?

A striking thing about Russia's invasion in Ukraine is that it had been more than 30 years since one country tried to invade another. The last case was that of Iraq in 1990, when it invaded Kuwait. Many thought these types of wars had long disappeared. But we can always be surprised by history, as the present convulsive time shows. In the words of Fazal (2022), "Now, with Russia's invasion, the norm against territorial conquest has been tested in the most threatening and vivid way since the end of World War II. The war in Ukraine is reminiscent of a previous, more violent era".

Borders have always been a symbol of sovereignty, but today this vision has been further reinforced. But in a globalized world shaped by uncertain times, this vision of sovereignty clashes with the necessity to find sustainable and safe ways to deal with migration more efficiently at the international level. Global governance – on migration and on any area – is strongly connected to the obedience of international norms. In a liberal world order, the law is one of the most important tools to maintain international peace. But instead, today we are witnessing a preference to deal with international issues through unilateralism. The widening of the security agenda, with new international threats destabilizing the safety of the citizen and the nation (as with the case of climate change, migratory movements, and terrorism, among others), has opened the creation of new threats, but it has also unsettled established mechanisms of global governance (Gaskarth, 2013). Repucci and Slipowitz (2022) are straightforward in this sense: "The global order is nearing a tipping point, and if democracy's defenders do not work together to help guarantee freedom for all people, the authoritarian model will prevail".

In a convulsive world and an era of change, the global community can still use the international legal framework to maintain an order based on democracy, liberties, and freedoms. Some norms are grounded in humanitarian concerns (such as that against genocide or ethnic cleansing), and other norms are based on maintaining stability (such as that against conquest). The prohibition to conquer is also a norm preventing major clashes, as many wars started precisely because of territorial controversies. The United Nations Charter encompasses all these norms, and it is a source to maintain peace and stability within the international order, while seeking greater international cooperation to solve global problems. The speech of Kenyan UN Ambassador Martin Kimani in 2022 at the UN Security Council still resonates:

> This situation echoes our history. Kenya and almost every African country was birthed by the ending of empire. Our borders were not of our own drawing. They were drawn in the distant colonial metropoles of London, Paris, and Lisbon, with no regard for the ancient nations that they cleaved apart. . . . Rather than form nations that looked ever backward into history with a dangerous nostalgia, we chose to look forward to a greatness none of our many nations and peoples had ever known. We chose to follow the rules of the Organisation of African Unity and the United Nations charter, not because our borders satisfied us, but because we wanted something greater, forged in peace.
>
> (Kimani, 2022)

Luckily, a wide range of states stand against the proliferation of wars and still uphold the norms embodied in the United Nations Charter. In addition, sanctions and international courts can try to redress the situation in Ukraine and Ghaza. The United Nations can undergo a series of changes to be influent again and keep its goals to maintain international peace and security. As Biersteker (2017) holds,

> In spite of all the disorder and complexity associated with global security issues, however, there is a great deal of purpose and authoritatively rule-governed order present in the contemporary international system. It is not always a very just or efficient system of governance, but is governance nevertheless, and is central to any understanding of attempts to address contemporary security challenges.

Along these lines, Ikenberry (2020) offers three potential solutions to maintain the Western liberal democratic model standing. He contends that one option is to make the liberal international order more friendly to China and Russia by promoting more "defensive" liberal principles such as self-determination, tolerance, and ideological pluralism. In this scenario, there would not have to be a single vision of a world liberal order, but a more conservative stance would be taken to accommodate diverging views. A second approach would be based on "offensive" liberalism, that is, a more aggressive tactic against illiberal states to push them towards regime change. In this case, the assumption would be that countries like China and Russia will always be a threat to the liberal internationalism and therefore, the only way for this to survive is to contend these opposing forces and suppress authoritarian regimes so that democracy can prevail. A third and last alternative would be a combination of the previous two. This mixed strategy would find ways to cooperate with China and Russia when dealing with common problems, while at the same time actively seeking to consolidate liberal democratic values and allies across the world.

On the opposite side of the spectrum, Mearsheimer, a realist par excellence, sees the decay of liberalism as inevitable. He understands the position of the United States in the world as being based on moments after the Cold War ended. The United States was so powerful that it became an uncontested hegemony, spreading its liberal values across the world, fostering an open international economy, and building international institutions. It wanted to span its own image over the globe, and it believed that a liberal world would be more peaceful and reduce global problems such as those in relation to nuclear conflicts or terrorism. However, he says, liberal hegemony was destined to fail, as this strategy "invariably leads to policies that put a country at odds with nationalism and realism, which ultimately have far more influence on international politics than liberalism does" (Mearsheimer, 2018).

However, this need not necessarily be the case. As Özkirimli (2023) argues, we are currently witnessing a setback of liberalism, but not its end. And that is because even in the most imperfect of democracies, they are still the only referent frame. What is most important to maintain the liberal order is that democratic forces confront "their own complicity in the retreat of liberalism and offer a new vision that breaks the cycle of indignation and polarization that paralyzes democratic institutions today".

This book has at times offered a rather pessimist view of the era of change in which we are living. It has studied the securitization of migration exploring the ways in which states have applied measures to contend migration, but it has also offered a new perspective on how these securitization processes show a setback for the liberal order. Nonetheless, this is not a realist book defending the irreversible relapse of the order that has prevailed since the end of the Cold War. Instead, it wants to expose the rise of practices prioritizing national security precisely to warn about their consequences that these may have on the international order as we know it. The securitization of migration has a clear negative impact on the rights of these groups. But it is also a warning sign that something greater is also at stake. And it is only by being aware of this threat that we can take action.

References

Aragó, L. (2022, March 17). La Guerra de Ucrania causa el éxodo de refugiados más rápido de la historia. *La Vanguardia*. Retrieved February 16, 2024, from www.lavanguardia.com/internacional/20220317/8130331/guerra-ucrania-causa-exodo-refugiados-mas-rapido-historia.html

Biersteker, T. (2017). Global security governance. In M. Dunn Cavelty & T. Balzacq (Eds.), *Routledge handbook of security studies*. Routledge.

Bigo, D., & Tsoukala, A. (2008). Understanding (in)security. In *Terror, insecurity and liberty. Illiberal practices of liberal regimes after 9/11*. Routledge.

Fazal, T. (2022, May/June). The return of conquest? Why the future of global order hinges on Ukraine. *Foreign Affairs*.

Gaskarth, J. (2013). Security and global governance. In S. Harman & D. Williams (Eds.), *Governing the world?* Routledge.

Ikenberry, J. G. (2020). The end of liberal international order? *International Affairs*, *94*(1), 7–23.

International Organization for Migration (IOM). (2021). Migration and migrants: A global overview. In *World Migration Report 2022*. Author. Retrieved February 15, 2024, from https://publications.iom.int/books/world-migration-report-2022

International Organization for Migration (IOM). (2024). *Missing migrants project*. Author. Retrieved February 19, 2024, from https://missingmigrants.iom.int

Kimani, M. (2022, February 21). Statement by Ambassador Martin Kimani, during the Security Council urgent meeting on the situation in Ukraine. *The Permanent Mission of the Republic of Kenya*. Retrieved February 15, 2024, from www.un.int/kenya/sites/www.un.int/files/Kenya/kenya_statement_during_urgent_meeting_on_on_ukraine_21_february_2022_at_2100.pdf

Mearsheimer, J. J. (2018). *The great delusion: Liberal drams and international realities*. Yale University Press.

Özkirimli, U. (2023). *El liberalism en retroceso*. Anuario Internacional CIDOB, Barcelona Centre for International Affairs. Retrieved February 17, 2024, from www.cidob.org/en/articulos/anuario_internacional_cidob/2023/el_liberalismo_en_retroceso

Repucci, S., & Slipowitz, A. (2022). The global expansion of authoritarian rule. *Freedom House*. Retrieved February 8, 2024, from https://freedomhouse.org/report/freedom-world/2022/global-expansion-authoritarian-rule

Saifi, Z. (2022, March 18). How the Ukraine war revealed Europe's selective empathy on refugees. *CNN*. Retrieved February 16, 2024, from www.cnn.com/2022/03/16/middleeast/mideast-summary-03-16-2022-intl/index.html

Townsend, M. (2022, March 19). Stranded Nigerians accuse UK of ignoring pleas of black refugees fleeing Ukraine. *The Guardian*. Retrieved February 16, 2024, from www.theguardian.com/world/2022/mar/19/stranded-nigerians-accuse-uk-of-ignoring-pleas-of-black-refugees-fleeing-ukraine

United Nations High Commissioner for Refugees (UNHCR). (2023a, October 24). *Refugee data finder*. Retrieved February 16, 2024, from www.unhcr.org/refugee-statistics/

United Nations High Commissioner for Refugees (UNHCR). (2023b). *Operational data portal. Refugee situations*. Retrieved July 7, 2023, from https://data.unhcr.org/en/situations

World Bank. (2023). *World development report 2023: Migrants, refugees and societies*. Author. Retrieved February 15, 2023, from www.worldbank.org/en/publication/wdr2023

Index

For Product Safety Concerns and Information please contact our EU
representative GPSR@taylorandfrancis.com
Taylor & Francis Verlag GmbH, Kaufingerstraße 24, 80331 München, Germany

www.ingramcontent.com/pod-product-compliance
Lightning Source LLC
LaVergne TN
LVHW021247011026
849160LV00010BA/945

* 9 7 8 1 0 3 2 6 0 2 2 2 6 *